Ian Sheppard
SPCK Book Sale
London   Jul. 74.

THE LIBRARY OF PRACTICAL THEOLOGY

General Editor : Martin Thornton

ONE PEOPLE, ONE CHURCH, ONE SONG

ONE PEOPLE,
ONE CHURCH, ONE SONG

by

JOHN MULLETT

HODDER AND STOUGHTON

Copyright © 1969 by John Mullett

First printed 1968

SBN 340 04329 6

Printed in Great Britain for Hodder and Stoughton Limited, St. Paul's House, Warwick Lane, London, E.C.4, by Ebenezer Baylis and Son, Limited, The Trinity Press, Worcester, and London

Acknowledgements

This work would never have been begun but for the learning
and encouragement of the Reverend R. P. Symonds, now
Vicar of St. Mary de Castro, Leicester, who sent me delving
into things musical and liturgical. That I have found the
psalms relevant is due to my training as a boy chorister under
Sir Ernest Bullock, from whom I learned much, both of the
principles of Christian worship, and of Christian living. The
Right Reverend Dr. C. Kenneth Sansbury, General Secre-
tary of the British Council of Churches, has generously given
of his time to read over the text and make careful observa-
tions on it.

It was on the farm of Mr. and Mrs. Jim Fowler in Central
Africa that the foundation work was done towards this book.
The quiet hospitality of their home in Que Que away from
rectory visitors and telephone was a great joy to me. In
thanking them, I must also thank a great host of good ladies
who have typed about psalms, and still more about psalms,
over a dozen or so years. In particular I am indebted to
Mrs. Winifred Fairfax Franklin, Mrs. Beryl Montgomery
and Mrs. Betty Challender, who have slaved beyond measure,
and to the Reverend Derek Smith and the Reverend John
Haynes, who as fellow labourers have made it possible for
me to complete this study.

BOLLINGTON
St. Peter's Day 1967   J. St. H. M.

Editorial Preface

During recent years there has been a remarkable revival of interest in theological studies, covering a wide range of thought and extending to an expanding public. Whatever its underlying causes, this movement has certainly been stimulated by some bold and radical speculation, as well as by a continuing quest for greater personal responsibility in theological decision.

Those responsible for *The Library of Practical Theology* welcome these trends, while recognising that they create new problems and make new demands. Our aim is to try to be of some service in meeting this new situation in a practical way, neither taking sides in current controversy nor forcing any particular viewpoint upon our readers. We hope, rather, to assist them to follow their own theological reasoning, and to interpret their own religious experience, with greater clarity. This implies a practical evaluation both of current scholarship and more popular religious thought, which in turn presupposes a certain amount of background historical theology. "A modern re-statement of traditional doctrine" necessitates a sympathetic understanding of what is being re-stated. "Contemporary trends" are hardly intelligible without some study of the historical process from which they have evolved.

A new theological interest having been awakened, we feel that the time is ripe to launch a series of this kind, and we hope that it proves not entirely false to all the implications of its title. We hope that it will develop into a true *Library*, a carefully planned corpus of practical studies and not just an interesting collection of books. By *Practical* we mean that which impinges on human experience and makes sense of the present situation. And, while avoiding the heavily technical, the Library will be unashamedly concerned with *Theology*. Our faith is that theology still holds the key to the ultimate meaning of the universe, and as the indispensable interpreter of religious experience, it is still the mainspring of the deepest human fulfilment.

MARTIN THORNTON

CONTENTS

chapter   *page*

    Acknowledgements   5
    Editorial Preface   7
    Foreword by Sir Ernest Bullock, C.V.O.,
      LL.D., MUS.D., F.R.C.M., F.R.C.O., HON. R.A.M.   13

One   A CONTEMPORARY OVERTURE   15
    Ark and Liturgy   15
    Ecumenical Liturgy   16
    Ordered Liturgy   18
    Mission and Liturgy   20
    Whose is the Liturgy?   22

Two   THE PSALMS ARE SONGS   26
    The Parish and its Prayer   26
    Cranmer, the Clerks and Evensong   28
    The Office is the Song   29

Three   ON THE PHILOSOPHY OF SOUNDS   32
    In Tune with God   32
    Psalm and Ecstasy   34
    The Holiness of Numbers   36
    The Age of Reason (and of Talk)   37
    The Age of Humanism   38

Four   "PSALMS AND HYMNS AND SPIRITUAL
    SONGS"   41
    The Spiritual Songs   41
    The Hymns   45
    The Psalms   47

Five   CHURCH AND SYNAGOGUE   53
    The Daily Word and the Daily Food   53
    The Authority of Scripture   55
    The Synagogue and the Parish Church   58
    The Tension of Transition   59

Six   CRANMER AND THE REFORM   63
               After the Primitive Hare   63
               The Medieval Psalter   65

Seven   ASPECTS OF THE OFFICE IN THE
           EIGHTEENTH CENTURY   68
               Altar and Font   68
               Community and Common Prayer   69
               A Time for Reform   72
               The Bishops' Call   73
               A Hymn to Help   75
               The Musicians' Offering   76
               "And Now the Merry Organ"   77

Eight   ASPECTS OF THE OFFICE IN THE
           NINETEENTH CENTURY   81
               The Survival of a Remnant   81
               The Laymen Speak Out   84
               The Oxford Movement and the Office   87
               Some Conclusions   90

Nine   PARSON, PEOPLE AND THE OPUS DEI IN
           THE TWENTIETH CENTURY   93
               The Laity and the Caviar   94
               Soul-starved Priests   96
               Sterile Performances   97
               Unshackle the Psalter   99

Ten   A PSALTER ARRANGED FOR SONG   102
               Revisions Compared   102
               The Daily Office Psalter   106
               The Eucharistic Psalter   107
               The Psalter for Saints and Occasional
                   Offices   109
               The Memory and the Spiritual Life   110
               Interpretation in the Wind of Change   116

Eleven   WORSHIP IN THE AGE OF DIN   121
              The Question of Silence   121
              Music and Productivity   123
              The World of Health and Education 124

Twelve   THEOLOGICAL CONSIDERATIONS IN
           LITURGICAL REFORM   127
              The Training of Men in Prayer   127
              The Musician Divorced   129
              The Cathedral Canon in the Twentieth
                 Century   131
              The Theology of the Cathedral Church
                 in the Twentieth Century   132
              The Liturgical Possibilities in the
                 Twentieth Century   134

Thirteen   CONCERNING "COMMON PRAYER"   144
              The Daily Office and the Community 144
              The Daily Office and the Layman   146
              The Daily Office in Solitude   148
              One People, One Church, One Song   151

Appendix   A TABLE OF PSALMS ARRANGED FOR
           COMMON PRAYER   153
              Psalms at Mattins   155
              Psalms at Evensong   159
              Psalms at the Holy Communion   163
              Psalms for Saints and Occasional
                 Offices   170
              Psalms for Private Recitation   173

Notes   174
Index   187

FOREWORD

by

SIR ERNEST BULLOCK

C.V.O., LL.D., MUS.D., F.R.C.M., F.R.C.O., Hon. R.A.M. sometime
Organist and Master of the Choristers, Westminster Abbey,
and Director of the Royal College of Music.

When John Mullett was a boy he was a chorister in the
Westminster Abbey choir during my time there as Organist
and Master of the Choristers. Consequently, many of the
opinions and matters discussed in this book no doubt were
being unconsciously formulated in his mind at that time.
After serving as an officer in the Royal Navy, and studying at
Cambridge University and Lincoln Theological College he
was ordained and worked as a parish priest near London, and
then in the Middle East and Africa, before becoming Vicar of
Bollington. Although a comparatively young man, his experience of pastoral and parish work has been wide, and,
since he is also an organist, his understanding of a church
musician's work is of additional value.

In the Church of England at the present time there are
many traditions, forms of worship and customs being re-
examined and changes contemplated, which will affect both
its liturgy and music. Readers of this book, which is the
result of the author's experience and qualifications, will be
well advised to heed his words.

A strong point is made of the importance of the psalms
and the need for retaining them in worship. Anyone who has
been accustomed to sing or recite the whole Psalter, as
ordained by the Book of Common Prayer, cannot fail to be
impressed by their aptness to everyday life, their high moral
tone, and the atmosphere they create for worship.

In a parish church, the incumbent is in charge of the style
of worship, but, as far as the music is concerned, it is doubtful

whether he is always sufficiently knowledgeable or ready to take advice as regards the practicability and suitability of the choice worthy to be offered in worship. It is a great temptation to use music merely to attract a congregation. This practice has been condemned from time immemorial and must still be strongly condemned. It matters not whether the music is good or bad, classical or avantgarde, "pop" or "jazz", if the motive is to attract the temptation must be resisted.

In a cathedral of the old foundation, the precentor, who is in charge of the music, ranks next to the dean. At one time this worked reasonably well because the precentor was chosen on account of his liturgical scholarship and musical ability. Later, the precentor's qualifications became less important, and the status of the office took precedence. In new foundations and more recent times, the precentor has lost his rank second to the dean or provost and is a minor canon, and not usually a member of the chapter.

In my own experience, I can think of no better man who was qualified in every way to hold the office of precentor than the late Bishop W. H. Frere. It was my great privilege to know him as a friend. Truly he was a remarkable soul, a saint, a great theologian and an authority on liturgiology and music, particularly plainsong; but what impressed me most was his profound humility. The revision of the 1928 Prayer Book owed much to Bishop Frere's scholarship and wise counsel, and those in charge of present day Prayer Book reforms would be well advised to study his works. Although I know that Mr. Mullett never had the good fortune to know Bishop Frere, yet it seems clear that the Bishop has influenced him, and it is devoutly hoped that others will follow the example of the author of this book.

LONG CRENDON, BUCKS.
May 31st 1967

CHAPTER ONE

A Contemporary Overture

The rope that the rats run up to get into a ship is the same rope that rats run down to get out of a ship.

ARK AND LITURGY

"The history which separates us from the Event of Christ, is also the indispensable nexus which *connects* us with that Event—and thus connects us with each other." A. C. Oulter wisely corrects our psychological approach to Christian unity and ecumenism.[1] Why must we always be so full of remorse about our "unhappy divisions"?[2] Since folk learn their faith from their public prayers and such phrases as this are constantly being put into their minds, we are not surprised to find that most people regard Christian disunity as an unhappy topic. The body of Christ must rejoice today about the vigour of life and flames of fire which reforms, and dare one say schisms, have carried. Oulter reminds us that as history has separated us, so it is history that unites us.

The rope which holds the ship—"the Ark of Christ's Church"—is the worship of the Church, in every age and in every division of the family. The rope is made of many strands. Above all, the common denominator of the rope and of worship is the Book of Psalms, or as the Fathers neatly put it, the singing of David. The monumental work of Rowland E. Prothero *The Psalms in Human Life* demonstrates how Catholic and Protestant, Russian and American, and all known Christian ethnic groups, have nurtured their souls on David.[3] I believe that as the rats ran up the rope they can also run down. I believe there is no greater vehicle of unity than the Psalter. I believe we should, in the Church of England, hasten to put this side of our own house in order. The psalms form the basis of our Book of Common Prayer. If we have anything in particular to offer the world, to the "one people",[4] it is the Book of Common Prayer. Many eminent people seem to think our contribution is to be the "mean between two extremes".[5] This puts Anglicans immediately in the position of being a "no people". The *Ecclesia Anglicana* has much more to offer to ecumenical debate than to be a mean. It must set in order and then offer its liturgy, in particular its biblical word and song. The Book of Common Prayer without the Psalter would be no more than a remnant of devotion.

ECUMENICAL LITURGY

Dr. W. R. Matthews, former Dean of St. Paul's, spoke with supreme clarity: ". . . if we really want to begin creating unity without delay we had better start with worship."[6] We have already started. Erik Routley has shown that if you picked up a hymn book in 1920 "you could tell in a couple of minutes by examining its contents whether it came from the Church of England or Dissent. In our time the only way you can distinguish between an Anglican and Dissenting book in plain covers is to check whether it contains 'Eternal Light' by Thomas Binney. If it doesn't it's Anglican."[7] We notice here no mention of the Roman Catholic tradition. Historically the greater unity in worship is in David not in hymns. Dr. J. A. Lamb in his essay on *Liturgy and Unity* tries to point the way ahead. To try and construct acts of worship which can be used in common tends to be an eclectic process. It results in being devoid of that which is the very essence of liturgy: "living tradition". Lamb quotes Roger Hazelton:

"What is needed is not a medley but a melodic line, not a patchwork but a pattern."[8]

To start with the eucharist, as so many want to do, is to attempt to get at the heart of the onion without removing the skin. Peel off first the outward dry layers of hatred and suspicion and then we are in a position to sing and pray together. This is historically the position at which we have now arrived through the prayers and labours of Pope John. To achieve the melodic line rather than the medley we must go to David. Here is ready made the chief vehicle of the daily office. If we can achieve some unity in David, then we are not far from being able to sing, as "one people", a daily office, despite differences in dogmatics and historical theology.

This approach to ecumenity is also found in Roman Catholic theologians. "Liturgical Reform and a concentration upon the practical aspects of pastoral care—these are important, positive features in all attempts towards reunion . . . it is quite possible for the Church to be renewed and for a positive forward thrust to be given to the movement towards a closer understanding between the various Christian communions, without previously clearing up every theoretical question." Hans Kung here thinks, as he often thinks, in the terms of a parish priest.[9] Dom Olivier Rousseau of Chevatogne is even more to the point. "It has seemed to me that something more could be done—by making use of the Psalter in an ecumenical psalmody in which all could share. All traditions see the Psalter as uniting and summarising the scriptures. Its task is now to bring all Christians together."[10]

Cardinal Cushing of Boston goes further: "One may perhaps envisage a time when all Christians and Jews may accept a common Psalter. How excellent it would be if the psalms could further unite all of us in some form of public recognition of the Judeo-Christian Tradition." Dr. Joseph Hertz, Chief Rabbi of England, complements such aspirations with his definition "They are the hymn book of humanity."[11]

It is this ideal that I have set before you in Chapter Ten. There, and in the table in the Appendix, I have tried to draw upon the riches of both the Roman and Anglican traditions. I have tried to include something of the custom of the Orthodox Churches, to bridge not only the historical usages and modern pastoral needs, but also to draw in the threads of early Jewish and Christian practices. For the unity of the "one people" of God which Westminster Abbey set before us in 1966, when celebrating the 900th anniversary of Dedication, is a unity deeper than sixteenth century political wrangles.

ORDERED LITURGY

Whilst it is true that the Anglican, with the Book of Common Prayer to use, is closer in form in his daily office to the Roman Catholic than to the Free Churchman, we welcome the much increased interest which Free Churches show in liturgy. Once, of course, the very idea of liturgical form was anathema. It was, according to John Owen, "the gilding of the poisonous pill, whose operation when it was swallowed, was to bereave men of their senses, reason and faith".[12] The question now has to be asked: why is it anathema? A considerable amount of Free Church writing in this century has encouraged formality in prayer. One asks "why is it thought right to use another's words in praise (a hymn) and not in prayer?"[13] Another can question whether there is not a psychological difficulty in the threefold exercise of (a) grasping the extempore prayer of the minister, (b) making it your own and (c) directing it at God.[14]

The more accustomed one is to the words of the prayer being offered, the easier it is actually to pray the prayer. This is because the mental process of listening has become less important. Dom Robert Petitpierre clarifies this operation.

The congregation has (a) to *hear* what is said, (b) to *think* what the phrase means and (c) to *turn* this meaning into prayer.[15]

The signs of the times point one way. If the Anglican can make his daily office work, many Free Churchmen will welcome it. Parts of the Book of Common Prayer are being used on Sundays in Nonconformist worship, and on week-days many ministers find the use of Common Prayer a valuable assistance to their ministry.

The great vehicle of worship is psalmody. We will need to demonstrate later that "psalmody is song". Ecumenity must stand aside for a while from the perpetual dogmatic debate of the intellectuals and let in the fresh air, with the songs of "The Sparrows of the Spirit"[16] singing together in David. The birds migrate and still sing the same song.

As long ago as 1877 W. Alexander drew our attention to the truly catholic nature of the Psalter: " . . . catholic in the sense that it is in use wherever the Gospel is preached and the sacraments are administered. Not a branch of the Church but uses it, and that in nearly every type of service . . . Every language, and every section of Christendom, has its own particular delight in the psalms. The awful pomp of the Latin Church; the homelier forms of Teutonic Christianity; the speculative subtlety and exuberant rhetoric of the Greek even before the altar; the sober and reserved reverence of the Anglican Church; the austere severity of sectarian devotion; find their expression in the Psalter."[17]

These words, written nearly a century ago, have still not been heeded. The old Jerusalem was built upon the ideology of the unity of the tribes centred upon the unity of David's city. "Thither the tribes go up" (Ps. 122 v. 4). The unity was in the person and family of David. Today the unity must be unearthed in and through the songs of David.

Dr. J. A. Lamb in his essay "Liturgy in Unity" demonstrates that the subjects of worship are the same in various traditions, i.e. that all derive in the main from Holy

Scripture. He continues: "The materials used for praise in the services are also a common possession of the whole Church. The use of the Psalter is obvious in this respect; for every section of the Church in every century of the Christian era has used this book with appreciation and joy. There is no kind of service however simple or elaborate that has altogether rejected the psalms. It is true there have been times and places when the Psalter has suffered neglect. The Roman services for example, both the daily offices and mass, in the process of time greatly reduced the amount of psalmody; but recently the desire has been expressed to put psalmody on a firmer foundation and to give it a larger place in worship."[18]

MISSION AND LITURGY

The Church must concern itself again with Mission, with no less enthusiasm than those who lived in the 1860s and 1870s. There were probably more martyrs of the Anglican Communion in the nineteenth century than in any other period of its history, not discounting the bloody reforming years of the sixteenth century. No doubt the opportunity for overseas mission and for martyrdom was created by the capitalist, who exported the iron railway lines of the Industrial Revolution, by the success of British troops in battle, and by the establishment of colonial empire. All of this the contemporary mind is apt mistakenly to dismiss as hypocritical and obnoxious.

There was a ceaseless, largely one way traffic of men and women to the newly found continents. Within a few years Bishop Mackenzie died on the river bank in Central Africa in 1862, Bishop Patterson in a lagoon in the South Pacific in 1871, Bishop Hannington in a dark hut in Uganda in 1885. The walls of St. Augustine's College, Canterbury, show how few years a man had to live who received his apostleship there. The Anglican Communion as it is today with its fine variety of liturgy and devotion in countless tongues, is in no small measure the fruit of the blood of these stiff Victorian characters. It was on St. Peter's Day 1847, when Bishop Gray was consecrated bishop of Capetown, and Perry, Short and Tyrell bishops of Melbourne, Adelaide and Newcastle, that the Abbey at Westminster took down its wooden screens across the transept to make room for the 760 communicants at a fully choral eucharist.[19]

Opportunity for mission is just as great today, but it is not linked with the railroad and the iron steamship. It is linked with the highway of the fast motor car, and with the tourist agency, with the business man from New York or from the quiet villages of the English countryside, who thinks nothing of being in Germany, or Japan or India this week, next week and the week after. Within the Church, Christian stewardship is helping to recreate a sense of responsibility for mission in a Church which to a large extent has ceased to be an "Apostolic" Church in any live sense at all. Few of the baptised have the slightest notion of apostolicity or mission.

The man who gets outside his village, outside his parish, either as a trade union leader or as a tourist, cannot but face the truth that mission today means the battle for values in the minds of the world's workers. It is irrelevant if they are making Fiats in Milan or Wolseleys in Oxford. Mission in Central Africa goes hand in hand with education. Mission in India with health and healing. The hospital and the schoolroom are the two features of twentieth century civilisation which are common to the "one people".

Rightly or wrongly, the Church thinks that since it gave these two benefits to European civilisation, it has the duty to give them also to other races and other religions. The Church thinks that it has a special reason for both educating the mind and healing the body. Atheists and agnostics regard this reason as superfluous or mythical.

Many open-eyed men and women are turning towards

humanism. There is a cry for holding forth to primary school children on the wonders of comparative religion. We must value it is said, what others have, and share it. The second Vatican Council meets this cry with the wisdom of allowing "adaptation of the Liturgy to different peoples".[20] The spirit to be "one people" is more and more, thus, to be "one people" in diversity; if only the Anglican desire to be part of the "one people" but a "different people" could have succeeded in the sixteenth century.

The Christian still believes he has a unique offering to make on the altar of sacrifice: an offering which no amount of education or healing can imprint by itself. The mission to the modern world is ludicrous as Christians pray and learn apart in their several ecclesiastical nests of bricks and cement. The mission will come from renewal, and renewal will come from common prayer. Above all, the clergy should learn to pray together and sing together, and this cannot wait. "The central point of renewal is the reform of religious worship, and it would be impossible to renew the Church, without renewing those who are in holy orders."[21]

WHOSE IS THE LITURGY?

Hans Kung goes on to propose a scheme for the renewal of worship for Roman Catholic priests. He looks for a daily office for the clergy who are engaged in pastoral work on much the same lines as Cranmer proposed and executed. Hans Kung however has less "time" in the twentieth century to offer day by day. He suggests forty-five minutes — a quarter of an hour for consecrative Bible reading, a quarter of an hour for meditation or modern spiritual reading. The third quarter goes to what remains necessary for a morning and evening daily office—psalms and prayer. No doubt only an hour a day is too radical for the twentieth century Anglican Prayer Book reformers. One point from Hans Kung must be grappled with. The Man of God must have "necessary time" to be with God when he is not frustrated by the prescribed "number of words".[22]

Before leaving this dynamic author, we note his reminder: "The hours of the Church then, began as voluntary and private prayer which was practiced by *all* the faithful." It is not until the European ecclesiastical culture of the twelfth century that the saying of pseudo-monastic offices was by rule imposed upon all the secular clergy. I hope to show that whatever reforms may be necessary to the Book of Common Prayer, they must be on the basis that that book is a book of *daily* prayer. Furthermore it was intended for daily use not for the salvation of the clergyman's soul but for "all the faithful". It was once said by "all the faithful"—*daily*.

There have been times when *Ecclesia Anglicana* has been proud of its Book of Common Prayer. It did after all translate it into Spanish in the seventeenth century. It wasn't hard then to persuade the Spaniards that there was no "savour of corruption of doctrine, much less of heresie . . . " This unusual translation was the result of the Welsh Puritan Dean Williams keeping in his house at Westminster the Dominican John Tuxeda. The Dean was glad to have the Roman Catholic Ambassador sitting in his church listening to his choir singing part of the English liturgy on the dark winter's night of December 15th 1624. The choir in copes, the court in evening dress, Orlando Gibbons at the organ: indeed it was an exquisite and typical "Westminster Abbey" occasion. Even if the Dean was "absolutely unprincipled and as slippery as an eel" he had the virtue that "he procured the sweetest music both for the organ and for the voices in all parts that ever was heard in an English choir". It was his will "that God might be praised with a cheerful noise in his Sanctuary . . . "[23]

If the Welsh Dean had no principles in his conduct he had the love of music in his bones. If he kept the Deanery of Westminster to himself as well as his parsonage, his prebendal stall and his bishopric, so that he became "a perfect diocese in himself", it was, as his charitable biographer says, that "he was loth to stir from that seat where he had command of such excellent music".[24]

Music has power. It has the power to heal, it has the power to calm. It has the power to seduce the beloved. It has the power to induce work. Music in the twentieth century has the power to unite the "one people" of God. Music is an *esperanto*. Music needs no translation. The voice of song is one all men can share. Today the musicians of international fame make their music from city to city regardless of race, colour or creed. When we live in a world where racial hatred is threatening us with inter-continental hatred in the not too distant future, is the Church to stand aside and let this great vehicle of common humanity lie idly by? The Church must sing and shout in thundering unison. If you can do nothing else, "O clap your hands together, all ye people . . . For God is the King of all the earth" (Ps. 47 v. 1, 7).

Theologians and liturgiologists are bedevilled today with eucharistic spirituality. Westward position or eastern position, altars here or there, architectural chaos, vestments Gothic or not so Gothic, these are the questions which agitate so many. The centre of reform ought to be the office and private spirituality. As in the primitive church, in the modern Church in most parts of the world the eucharist by force of circumstances is an occasional and special service. The office, on the other hand, is a daily business. It was originally interlocked with Jewish contemporary and homely habit. We must *first* straighten out our prayer life and reform its relationship to Sunday church.

The daily routine of worship carried out in the great cathedrals of England and the prayers offered daily in the parish churches have ceased, in large measure, to be genuine prayer. A great artificiality in worship suffocates and causes the inertia which everywhere is so apparent. In the newer continents liturgies are springing up and the quiver could

soon become too full. In many ways the Church of England
has a better starting point from which to progress successfully
towards an ordered liturgy than the younger and more
buoyant parts of the Anglican family of Churches.

To be part of the great congregation of many races,
colours and indeed creeds in Westminster on the occasion
of the 900th Feast of Dedication of the Abbey Church on
December 27th 1965 was to realise that the Church can rise
beyond the narrowness of ecclesiastical frictions and petty
historical theological doctrinettes. The Church must take off,
become airborne, in this age. It needs both the courage of the
pilot and the brain of the technician. The first step towards
"one people" is the step of ecumenical relationships. As
H. G. Hageman has put it: "The fact remains that the
Liturgy is the most fruitful area for ecumenical exploitation.
If that fact is recognised and, in the best sense of the word,
exploited, we shall know what the next step may be."[25]

CHAPTER TWO

The Psalms are Songs

In the last century the Oxford Movement brought to life the eucharistic service, together with a revival of the dignity and beauty of worship. The Royal School of Church Music and the Parish and People Movement are both heirs to this tradition. In this century we find ourselves face to face with the duty of bringing to life the daily office (the *opus Dei*) which indeed is just as dead to us as the old monthly or quarterly said celebration of holy communion was to our forefathers in the last century. On Sundays many of us know that our parish communion has at least half wrecked the *opus Dei*, and on weekdays most clergy find themselves muttering faithfully to themselves the words of the offices within the parish churches in a manner far remote from anything Cranmer had in mind when they were shaped.

THE PARISH AND ITS PRAYER

George Addleshaw, Dean of Chester, concludes his tract *The Early Parochial System and the Divine Office*, with a plea for a "modern adaptation" of the first foundation parish churches. "The Church today," he says "faces many problems, similar to those which confronted it in the dark ages. Men and women have to be delivered from a secularism which is just as deadly to both soul and body as the old heathenism, and brought to find their real home in Christ's body. This pastoral problem manifests itself in particular in new housing areas owing to the rootlessness and lack of tradition and fewness of priests available compared with the vast size of the population."[1]

The "modern adaptation" would be staffed by a body of clergy and lay helpers, living as a community under some form of rule, with the addition of nuns as well; part being responsible for the parish work, part supporting that work by a life of prayer, intercession and special forms of self-denial. "It would be a new type of religious life to meet modern needs . . . At the heart of the parish the powers of evil, which walk abroad to devour men's souls, would be fought by a continuous offering of prayer and intercession. That prayer would include the public recitation of the daily prayers of the Church *in a form in which the parish could join.*"

What Dean Addleshaw wishes to see, a corporate worship in parish churches, is now only at the beginning. Here and there choirs are singing the odd weekday evensong in the parish churches, and the laity are being taught worship as the centre of the Church's business. The faithful laity are ready in small numbers to respond to the call to join in the *opus Dei*, but our drabness keeps them out.

The problem is not peculiar to the housing estates of overcrowded Britain. The writer, who has come from an African missionary parish, finds that while we have in the larger mission centres something akin to the old parochial organisation, the *opus Dei* is lacking in its fulness. Where there is a priest, the eucharist is usually offered daily. In these centres are gathered priests, schoolmasters, hospital staff, schoolchildren etc., much after the manner of the old foundations. The young African schoolmaster goes out into the bush from these centres, with no desire to go on singing the psalms day by day. He has a profoundly musical people to which he goes, but little to take them beyond a smattering of hymns after the manner of the Methodists for use on Sundays. We Church of England folk pride ourselves on maintaining the traditions and faith of the early Catholic

missionaries of England, but how different our methods are
to those of Patrick, Columba or Aidan. If these men sang
their psalters daily we may be sure their pupils walked out
across the hills with the words of the office upon their lips.
Our failure in the mission field is a failure in our home
grounding. We can only give what we have been given.

CRANMER, THE CLERKS AND EVENSONG

Whilst Cranmer laboured to bring the liturgy to the people,
in one way the very reform took it away from them. Every
church had had its singing man or men in addition to the
priest. It would appear that the general sweep out of the
treasury, jewels, choir books and ceremonial impedimenta
during the reign of Edward VI ended in leaving the clerk
only half a job of work. By 1671 John Playford was com-
plaining that in a hundred parish churches in the City of
London few clerks can sing properly; that they are chosen
more for poverty than for skill in music, and that God's
service is now brought into "Scorn and derision by many
people".[2] The clerk who was once the priest's continual aid,
in and out of service time, after being the black gowned
monster in the lower tier of the pulpit, ends up as the
present day verger sweeping up confetti. The *opus Dei* he
once performed shares likewise a degradation.

"It was Cranmer's aim . . . to recover as much as possible
of the worship of what he called the 'Primitive Church' "
(Lambeth 1958: 2. 80). *We suffer from uncompleted Cranmer.*
Cranmer's and Addleshaw's concern is this: "That prayer
will include the public recitation of the daily prayers of the
Church in a form in which the parish may join."

Arthur Bryant tells us in *The Makers of the Realm* that
Dunstan and his Benedictines made England famous for its
music.[3] Where is the "Singing Church" today? Its composers and choirs are too often engaged in fancy anthems to
the detriment of the liturgy and the *opus Dei*. Our congre-

gations are placid and effeminate. Do they not long for the
moment when, the *opus Dei* over, they may join more
effectively in the popular hymn which follows?

What a degradation it is when the Archbishop's Committee on Church Music reports in 1951, that in small
parishes where choirs are lacking "it is recommended that
the psalms should be read . . . It may be a regrettable fact,
but it has to be admitted that the psalms, whether they be
sung to plainsong or to Anglican chants, do not lend themselves readily to singing by the average congregation."[4]
What Church is this? Are not the psalms the Church's book
of songs? It is just as much nonsense to say David, as it
would be to sing Hamlet on a monotone. Indeed certain
numbers are relaxed and are reasonable in the spoken
voice, but the book as a whole *must be sung*.

"The difference between singing and reading a psalm
will easily be understood," wrote William Law (1686–
1761), "if you consider the difference between reading and
singing a common song that you like. Whilst you only read
it, you only like it, and that is all; but as soon as you sing it,
then you enjoy it, you feel the delight of it; it has got hold
of you, your passions keep pace with it, and you feel the
same spirit within you that seems to be in the words.

"If you were to tell a person that has such a song, that he
need not sing it, that it was sufficient to peruse it, he would
wonder what you meant; and would think you as absurd as
if you were to tell him that he should only look at his food,
to see whether it was good, but need not eat it: for a song of
praise not sung, is very like any other good thing not made
use of."[5]

THE OFFICE IS THE SONG

The change in title in 1952 from evensong to evening prayer
is symbolic of a change in stress throughout the whole Book
of Common Prayer. The intellectual element of Bible study

and sound theology has displaced the natural and emotional joys of simple worship. A vast armoury of minute changes in the Prayer Book between 1549 and 1662 can be produced to show how *song* was going from the Church. After the Restoration, anthems and similar secular entertainments begin to fill the void. We still suffer the pain.

The Church had always made the psalms its songs. "If we keep vigil in the Church David comes first and last and midst," says St. Chrysostom.

Adam of St. Victor puts it well in his sequence for the dedication of a church:

> "In the beginning (under the old covenant)
>   the trumpets sounded loud for that feast
> In the end (under the new covenant)
>   this is fulfilled through the Psalter."[6]

Alas, today we have swung back, for our rich churches have fine trumpets (inside organs) but the new song is lacking.

According to St. Athanasius: "We must not omit to explain the reasons why words of this kind should be not merely said but rendered with melody and song; for there are actually some simple folk amongst us, who, though they believe the words to be inspired yet think the reason for singing them is to make them more pleasing to the ear! This is by no means so; Holy Scripture is not designed to tickle the aesthetic palate, and it is rather for the soul's own profit that the psalms are sung. This is so chiefly for two reasons. In the *first* place it is fitting that the sacred writings should praise God in poetry as well as prose because freer, less restricted forms of verse, in which the psalms together with the canticles and odes are cast, ensures that by them men should express their love to God with all the strength and power they possess. And secondly the *reason* lies in the unifying effect which chanting the psalms has upon the singer. For to sing the psalms demands such concentration of a man's whole being on them, that, in doing it, his usual disharmony of mind and corresponding bodily confusion is resolved."[7]

The Book of Revelation gives a fine picture of every tongue and people and nation singing in a great chorus a new song (Rev. 7. 9). Today would we not want to substitute a democratically elected chamber for discussion, as our idea of heaven?

William Law wanted those who answered his *Serious Call* to sing daily in their prayers. He suggested that before beginning the psalm one might think "of all nations and kindreds and people and tongues, standing before the throne . . ." and then let the imagination follow until "it has placed you amongst those heavenly beings, and made you long to bear a part in their eternal music".[8]

He wanted the children to sing in the daily office in church. He wanted the servants and others who had no personal privacy nor opportunity in the daily office to sing aloud at their work. Without song there could be no joy or thanksgiving in Christian living and so he devotes a whole chapter to the "Chanting, or singing of Psalms in our private devotions".

In 1662, our Reverend Fathers in God at Savoy kept Coverdale for us, because it was "smoother" and "more easy to sing".[9] So let us sing and sing daily.

C. S. Lewis is so refreshing for a "modern". "What must be said," he says, "is that the psalms are poems, and poems intended to be sung; not doctrinal treatises, not even sermons."[10]

CHAPTER THREE

On the Philosophy of Sounds

IN TUNE WITH GOD

Paul knew enough philosophy as well as rabbinics to be no narrow bigot. "I am debtor both to the Greeks, and to the Barbarians" (Rom. 1. 14). If the sermon on the Areopagus was a failure as missionary theology, it shows us nevertheless that Paul inescapably had to come to terms with Gentile forms of religious expression. "For in him we live, and move, and have our being; as certain also of your own poets have said." (Acts 17. 28).

The man who is going to think about liturgy and worship in the twentieth century cannot afford to be an ostrich and assume that western Christendom has a monopoly of the science of prayer. Egyptians prayed before Christians and were possibly more vocal in prayer than Hebrews. The Egyptian lyre dates from 2000 B.C. and in the earliest examples it is found in the hands of the priests.[1] The sacred caste of Brahmins were originally singers of hymns. African spirituality keeps close to the drum and the dance and the Englishman rings the passing bell to keep the evil spirits off. The missionary technique is always to take, use and sanctify rather than to destroy. (Hence the western practice of celebrating the Lord's birthday on December 25th.)

Music is at the origin of religious expression. It must be taken and used, just as the Hebrews returned from the Captivity in Babylon and enhanced the worship of the rebuilt Temple with the greater sounds and greater colour and drama that they had learned in Babylon. The Christian must take the high science of the modern western orchestra and hallow it; and the African rhythms and hallow them; but he must also remember that man, just plain man, must sing to pray unless he is constantly a depressive. Even Paul and Silas had to sing in chains and nobody can say Paul was the jovial sort. Our 1662 Book of Common Prayer is too closely tied to Adam and his apple and the fact of sin. One must find God before one finds sin.

The doctrine of atonement has been sunk deep in human sin since Anselm. It may be that in this space age we must think again of attunement rather than atonement. The Greeks thought that the World Soul and the human soul could be in conformity; that music was bestowed upon mankind as a gift from heaven for the sake of harmony. Nicomachus of Gerasa ascribes to Pythagoras the discovery that the perfect consonances are expressible in terms of the ratios of the numbers one, two, three, four. Harmony, the blending or combining of opposites, becomes thus part of the order of things.[2] If the order of things today is mainly in the hands of the natural scientist, the physicist and the mathematician, we may be forgiven for asking the reader to take seriously the thought of Jesus as the Son of God to bring attunement to mankind. Aristotle could say the whole heaven is "a harmonia and a number".[3]

Music therefore can bring atonement—"the peace of God, which passeth all understanding".[4] David tried to bring it upon Saul with his harp. David failed where that popular priest musician from St. Catharine's College, Cambridge, John Bacchus Dykes, might well have succeeded. What attunement has been fulfilled in the hearts of men by the singing of his tune "Melita" to "Eternal Father":

"O Holy Spirit, who didst brood
Upon the waters dark and rude,

And bid their angry tumult cease,
And give, for wild confusion, peace."

Or again, who can say what obscurity might have befallen
that great hymn by the Bishop of Calcutta on the Trinity
had not Dykes been able to give it the melody and harmony.
Academically it may be inferior, but nevertheless it has
brought attunement between Christian men and women
of the nineteenth and twentieth centuries, and the Blessed
and Glorious Trinity.

"Holy, Holy, Holy! though the darkness hide Thee,
Though the eye of sinful man Thy glory may not see,
Only Thou art Holy, there is none beside Thee,
Perfect in power, in love, and purity."

Atonement comes then not only with repentance, with
the sacrifice of a scapegoat, but also with attunement. If
attunement happens in the course of an act of public
worship, then the purpose of the blessing is to pronounce that
this is so. Those who today think we get blessed too much
and who want to send the people out of church filled with
the Holy Spirit, dynamically entering into secular society,
propelled out through the main door, must remember that
the world needs both kinds of Christians. The introvert
and the extrovert have their places. Public worship must
resolve in individual at-one-ment. The words of the blessing,
"the peace of God," are intended to send men home atoned,
attuned, and in harmony with the "groaning creation" and
with God (Rom. 8. 22).

PSALM AND ECSTASY

The Hebrews made no pretence of being able to get at
Jahweh without music. "But now bring me a minstrel. And
it came to pass, when the minstrel played, that the hand of

the Lord came upon him" (2 Kings 3. 15). Elisha needed
the minstrel as Saul had done. If Michal was distressed at
her husband dancing before the ark it may well have been
that she "deplored the loss of self control among the men of
her family".[5] The twentieth century churchman is quite
happy to offer up the 150th psalm in a quasi-sacred, mediocre
manner allowing perhaps the organist to have the opportunity of parting with maximum wind. Michal knew too
much about the snags of timbrels and dances, strings and
pipe.

The indwelling spirit must surge as well as soothe. Saul
was told to meet the prophets on the road: "the Spirit of
the Lord will come upon thee, and thou shalt prophesy
with them, and shalt be turned into another man. And let it
be, when these signs are come unto thee, that thou do as
occasion serve thee; for God is with thee" (1 Sam.
10. 6, 7).

The power of music was used to incite a state of ecstasy,
in which the victim felt himself face to face with God as
Jacob had also felt himself muscle to muscle with God. Dr.
Guillaume argues that the dervish of the Middle East is the
natural successor to this line of devotion. In such phrases as
"shall . . . appear before the presence of God" in Psalm 42,
we see a later recension of what had previously been "appear
before the face of God!" The intimate anthropomorphic
deity gives way to the presence in the Temple in Jerusalem,
where the function of music is not to overcome but to
transport the mind. We move from the rhythm of the
prophet to the music of the mystic. Perhaps in this quotation
from the Mishna we see the marriage of the two. "Men of
piety and men of might used to dance before them with
burning torches in their hands, singing songs and praises.
And countless Levites (played) on harps, lyres, cymbals, and
trumpets and instruments of music, on the fifteen steps
leading down from the Court of the Israelites to the Court of
the Women, corresponding to the fifteen Songs of Ascents

in the Psalms; upon them the Levites used to stand with instruments of music and make melody."[6]

The Hebrew mystical tradition is carried on in the writings of Algazel in the tenth century. In the eighth chapter of his great book the *Ikya Ulum Al-din* he tells us that "the greatest joy which music brings is the privilege of the saints of God. The man who loves God passionately and longs to meet Him cannot look upon a thing but he sees it in Him, and he hears *every sound from Him and in Him*. Such a man is stirred by music to a passionate longing and love of God so that his heart, as it were, bursts into flame."[7]

But here we have the spirit of the psalmist rather than the prophet, for as Dr. Guillaume says, "To the Psalms rather than the Prophets we must turn for light on the Hebrews' desire for intercourse with God as an individual experience."[8] The psalms are the songs of the people of God, with or without band.

THE HOLINESS OF NUMBERS

"Personal religion is derived from ecstasy, theology from mathematics . . ." An astute comment from a great twentieth century mind, Bertrand Russell.[9]

The Church is indeed a debtor "both to the Greeks, and to the Barbarians" (Rom. 1. 14). Pythagoras was led to his mathematics through the medium of sound, of harmonics, of ratios, and sensitivity to balance and measure. If music is the father of numbers, and mathematics father of theology, then God must be a perfect concord! This, of course, solves the Bishop of Woolwich's problem of where God has gone, for he never was, except within—in the depth.[10] Instead of being a kind of super Daddy he is really a kind of super "ding" to which all other "dongs" are concordantly related. When the "dong" has become an ill-sounding unresonant "dung", this equals sin.

Here we are in the midst of the true psychology of the

musician who understands his medium to be a spiritual art, a craft intangible, so much superior to that of the sculptor who needs to handle his cosmic stone. He, the musician, unlike the men who labour and sweat and toil in the earth "to till the ground" (Gen. 3. 23), has no need of earthly things—he works in characters of depth. His purpose is "to give impressions of unknown things" as Edmund Gurney put it in *The Power of Sound* in 1880.[11]

Before we get hopelessly lost in the song of the Church, disappearing like the Lord in a cloud, or through the medieval height of the Angel Choir of Lincoln Minster, or in the welter of sound pouring through the bloodstream at the end of Beethoven's Ninth Symphony, let us come back quickly to Pythagoras. From him, his sound, and then his sums, comes in turn the glory of the Greeks, and also the *Summa* of Aquinas, so also the reasoning of Descartes, and the full mainstream of western theological doctrine. Pythagoras said "all things are numbers", and so led somebody else to say "In the beginning was the Word". Indeed Bertrand Russell is quite accurate: "Personal religion is derived from ecstasy, theology from mathematics . . . " Theology *is* derived from mathematics. Mathematics is certainly a department of music. Music and theology go hand in hand.[12]

THE AGE OF REASON (AND OF TALK)

Alas, since John Locke (1632–1704) propounded that "The great and chief end of men uniting into commonwealths, and putting themselves under government, is the preservation of their property" we have endured a spate of equality. We move on to "one man, one vote" and think this comes from the Acts of the Apostles where "the lot fell upon Matthias" and he was enabled to take his seat (Acts 1. 26). Modern man is obsessed with the democratic notion of society. The spoken word, the voice of the people, is unceasingly heard. The liturgy of 1662 fortunately predated the Reform Bill but it still reeks of words and the era of talk. The joy of the sound of God is lost in too many words. Addleshaw comments: "The lengthy readings from scripture, and the exhortations which form a large part of the Prayer Book rite, seem to lay a disproportionate emphasis on instruction."[13]

There are signs that in this age of nuclear science and space travel men's minds are being taken away from the political and spoken forum. "Who, that truly perceives the harmony of the Intellectual Realm could fail, if he has any bent towards music, to answer to the harmony in sensible sounds? What geometrician or arithmetician could fail to take pleasure in the symmetrics, correspondences, and principles of order observed in visible things?" This reflects something of the mind of the Cambridge Cavendish Laboratories in the mid twentieth century as well as being the mind of Plotinus when he wrote the *Enneads*.

THE AGE OF HUMANISM

The great medieval song schools with the monastic houses carried on the soul of the song of the Church while some fought and others slaved, but these latter also knew something of the sound of God, despite the clash of steel and the shouldering of burdens. It took cosmic form in both the chantry and the cathedral. But later the marriages of Church and state, of philosophy and priesthood, ruptured. "Art has left the heart of the temple and broadened out, has had to seek in the outside world the stage for its noble manifestations. How often—indeed how much more often— music must acknowledge the people and God as its source of life, must hasten from one to the other, to ennoble, comfort, and chasten mankind, and to bless and praise God." Franz Liszt writing in 1834 *On the Church Music of the Future*, having understood the unholy divorce and lamented the decline of religion, goes on: "To reach this goal, it is indispensable that a new music be invoked. This music, which for lack of another designation we may call humanistic (humanitarian), should be solemn, strong and powerful; it should unite in colossal relationships the theatre and the Church; it should be at the same time dramatic and holy, splendidly unfolding and simple, ceremonious and earnest, fiery and unbridled, stormy and restful, clear and fervent ... This will be the *fiat lux* of art."[14]

After all this we may be left wondering whether Franz Liszt was really more clear about his kind of God than John Robinson is of his. His prophecy however was fulfilled. There came in that very year (1834) "the Royal Musical Festival" in Westminster Abbey—"colossal relationships of the theatre and the Church." The century was full of "unbridled" sound. *Parsifal* in 1882 could show the blessed sacrament, the Redeemer, the sword and the wound on the stage with a fairy tale castle and tempting maiden. Meanwhile, "Curled up half asleep in their easy chairs, these enthusiasts let themselves be carried away or rocked to and fro by the pulsations of sound, instead of considering it with sharpened attention. As it more and more increases, subsides, exalts, or dies away, it transports them into an indefinite state of feeling which they are so innocent as to consider spiritual. They form the 'most grateful' public, and the one that is fit to discredit most surely the value of music." Eduard Hanslick writing in 1854 *On the Beautiful in Music: A Contribution to the Revival of Musical Aesthetics* gives a fair picture of the Wagner public.[15] Meanwhile in England oratorios take over the musical world in Leeds and Bradford and every little coal or cotton town. The marriage of the secular and the sacred takes place sometimes in the town hall, sometimes in the parish church. The sound of music is the same. How they enjoy it!

John Stainer's *The Crucifixion* (1887) forms the apex. Here we find Church and Chapel united, the cathedral with the tabernacle, the rich with the poor. Music, theatre music, that the people—yes, the 1832 Reformed People, the voting public—could accept, perform and love with a strange passion. The sound they could interpret, the words were working men's words.

Let us return to Franz Liszt and examine his prophetic adjectives in the light of Wagner and Stainer. The new music will need to be "humanistic", "solemn", "strong and powerful", will "unite in colossal relationships the theatre and the Church", will be "dramatic", "holy", "cere-monious", "unbridled", "clear and fervent".

Now the twentieth century teenager wants to know just why music must be solemn. Is God slow like all his hymns? Has he nothing in common with the age of the jet engine or the space rocket? Is he really so old and pompous, or shall we say "ceremonious"? What the neo-intellectual of the twentieth century wants is not this ecclesiastical flair for Elizabethan airiness in all the best places any more than a "humanism" that yearns for an age of elegance in a post war, dirty and somewhat sexually septic age. The sweeping thrills of the Service of Nine Lessons from the chapel of King's College, Cambridge, on Christmas Eve—is this the slip of a girl in the hand of God giving birth in a back street? *"Gloria in excelsis Deo"*; or is it *"Humanitas in excelsis"*? Perhaps it is both.[16]

CHAPTER FOUR

"Psalms and Hymns and Spiritual Songs"

St. Paul's exhortation to sing to yourselves in "psalms and hymns and spiritual songs" in Ephesians 5. 19 is often expounded from the pulpit as a long winded way of saying "sing up". Dr. Egon Wellesz now makes it quite clear that Paul tells us much more than this.

In the first place we should note the remarkable similarity between Ephesians 5. 19 and Colossians 3. 16. The former has "speaking to yourselves in psalms and hymns and spiritual songs, singing and making melody in your heart to the Lord". The latter has "teaching and admonishing one another in psalms and hymns and spiritual songs, singing with grace in your hearts to the Lord".

If Ephesians was in fact written by Paul, then he is clearly using on two occasions a technical or well used expression. If Ephesians was not written by Paul, then the author is either using the identical technical phrase or is himself prepared to copy exactly professional terminology.

These terms ψαλμοι ὑμνοι και ὠδαι πνευματικαι have been discussed by expositors ever since Origen, Basil and Augustine.

THE SPIRITUAL SONGS

Paul differentiates between songs and spiritual songs (ὠδαι πνευματικαι). The jubilant character of the latter sets it apart from ordinary odes. It is to be associated closely with "gifts of the Spirit" or with περι δε των πνευματικων, of 1 Corinthians 12. 1 etc.

We find the pentecostal outbursts at Corinth lead Paul to a considerable exhortation to the Church to be in discipline and order over its worship and its meetings (1 Corinthians 12). The next chapter begins "Though I speak with the tongues" and then Paul compares this with the pagan musical form "sounding brass, or a tinkling cymbal". In Colossians 3 Paul is concerned with the same indiscipline in worship. Be "forbearing", "forgiving"; "if any man have a quarrel—let the peace of God rule in your hearts". In Ephesians 5 we find similarly "walk circumspectly", "be not drunk", and in both passages the Church is exhorted to give thanks. The spiritual odes were therefore something which later expositors failed to experience in the course of normal worship. They disappear, as the speaking with tongues and improper disorders disappear from routine order.

In Augustine's time they still understood this liturgical use. On Psalm 99 he says "He who jubilates, speaks no words; it is a song of joy without words". Wellesz says: "The spiritual songs of which Paul speaks, were obviously the melismatic melodies, the Allelujas and other exultant songs of praise, which again, the Jewish Christians brought with them from the Temple and the Synagogue into the Christian Church . . . This view is supported by the musical structure of the Alleluias of the Ambrosian Rite, the oldest specimens of the type which survive in manuscripts."[1]

What concerns us here is that the 1662 Prayer Book rigidly removes all chances of ὠδαι πνευματικαι (spiritual songs), the singing for joy. All must be sung for intellectual improvement. Cranmer and the bishops of his generation were intoxicated with their discoveries in the Greek text and the words of the Fathers. It was an age of academic brilliance and from childhood the rigours of careful study and scholarship were pressed upon them. Cranmer entered Jesus College, Cambridge, at the age of fourteen, and his anonymous biographer (between 1556–1599) says he was "nossled in

the grossest kind of sophistry, logic, and philosophy moral
and natural, not in the text of the old philosophers, but
chiefly in the dark riddles and quiddities of Duns and other
subtle questionists". After eight years of this he took his
B.A. degree. With what joy did he turn to the intellectual
fresh air that blew into Cambridge with the reading of
Erasmus, whom he followed in his studies for his Master's
degree.[2]

Good as this was for Cranmer and the Church of England,
the removal of the Alleluias from the psalms and their
replacement by "Praise ye the Lord" has resulted in the
congregation at prayer not even knowing of the nature of
the "Hallel Psalms" (146–150). Had the Coverdale Psalms
given way to the Authorised Version of 1611, and had the
musicians really discovered the form, they might have done
something with "Praise ye the Lord". None of these things
happened and the "Hallel Psalms" now sit alongside the
penitential psalms and are far, far removed from being acc-
laimed fore and aft with a "spiritual song", an ᾠδὴ πνευματικη.
(The Revised Psalter, 1963 makes a provision, but the
printers and musicians have taken no notice and destroyed
the intention).

Within the set formula of the offices there are other
deficiencies of a similar but more serious nature.

The opening cry of the 1549 office had some ring of the
spiritual ecstasy that was once there. After the unfortunate
imposition of the "Pater Noster" in a "Loud Voice" came
the call to open lips and show praise. This, of course, was
not repeated at evensong when you had been (as we say in
the North of England) "mythering all day". In 1549, the
priest is ordered to say the *Gloria* in its entirety. To split the
Gloria as was done in 1662 into a versicle and response has
an unfortunate musical result. Who would think of playing
the first half of an overture with the woodwind and the
second half on the strings?

The Elizabethan musicians knew quite well what was

intended and got on with it. William Byrd (1543–1627) gives us a fine *Gloria* sung in five parts by the choir with a double "Praise ye the Lord" in full five parts to wind up. Thomas Tallis (1505?–1585) and Orlando Gibbons (1583–1625) do very much the same, while Thomas Tomkins (1575–1656) writes his "Praise ye the Lord" into the *Gloria* without a break.[3]

In 1662 the congregation lost even their little fling at Alleluia which 1549 provided for them from Easter to Trinity. The greater forty days begin to sink into the humdrum of routine Trinity or Ferial Sundays. Such remnants of "spiritual songs" (ὠδαι πνευματικαι) disappear from ordered liturgy and in the twentieth century people look to the Pentecostal sects for religious ecstasy. (What is true here of the *Gloria* and the Alleluia is to some degree matched by the history of the Hosanna in the *Sanctus* at the eucharist.)

We have been severely critical of the theologians who have taken from the musicians their opportunity of ecstatic sound at the calling of the Lord at the beginning of the office. It is well here to match the blame. The musicians still leave us to sing the inverted Alleluia "Praise ye the Lord. The Lord's Name be praised" to the same old Latin chant. Good for the Latin ending indeed, but quite hopeless in English when the ecstasy ends on a low note with a strong word in the dominant of the key.

We have digressed a long way from St. Paul and we must turn back to see what he meant by "psalms and hymns" as well as "spiritual songs".

THE HYMNS

Hymns were to suffer an early eclipse. Writings which were thought not to be authentically apostolic were excluded from the Canon in the fourth century. In the same way, in the fourth century the orthodox reacted against the words of hymns which could not be found directly in the text of scriptures (cf. the Council of Laodicaea, Canon 59).[4] This helps to explain why so few early hymns have survived. We may hazard a guess that Ephesians 5. 14 is a hymn remnant:

> "Wherefore he saith,
> Awake thou that sleepest,
> And arise from the dead,
> And Christ shall give thee light."

Possibly also 1 Tim. 3. 16:

> "God was manifest in the flesh,
> justified in the Spirit,
> seen of angels,
> preached unto the Gentiles,
> believed on in the World,
> received up into glory."

In the Pastoral Epistles and the Apocalypse there seem to be liturgical phrases which may have been in essence hymns, for example Revelation 5. 11 (N.E.B.):

> "Worthy is the Lamb,
> the Lamb that was slain,
> to receive all power and wealth,
> wisdom and might,
> honour and glory and praise!"

Working our way into the period of fixed liturgy, hymns that survive into formal use are the φως ιλαρον ("Hail, gladdening Light") and the Δοξα εν υψιστοις θεω (the western *Gloria in Excelsis*). These still represent the evening and morning hymns respectively for the daily evening and morning office of Eastern Orthodox worship.

A similar restriction on free hymnody was expressed by the Calvinists. It found its way into the Reformation stewpot and left the Book of Common Prayer almost hymnless. The remnants of hymnody remaining are the *Gloria in Excelsis* and the *Veni Creator*. The daily office has only the *Te Deum* as a true Christian hymn. One must always remember that in singing biblical canticles as Christian hymns a certain dexterity of mind is always required, as in psalmody. Despite the theological pressure the door could not be shut on natural hymnody, and Bishop Ken (only fourteen years after the publication of the 1662 Prayer Book) had to fill the void for his Winchester boys, giving them in *The Manual* "Awake, my soul, and with the sun". It was not, of course, intended to be sung by respectably dressed people on Sundays at the 11 a.m. mattins, but daily at the dawn of the light.[5] From here hymnody runs riot (see further Chapter Six).

We must now turn to developments in the Eastern Church. After the Council of Constantinople in 381 the persecution of the Monophysites forced the latter into song. Justinian, wishing to secure firm ecclesiastical authority throughout the empire, built the great Church of St. Sophia. It took 10,000 craftsmen four years. It was consecrated on December 27th 537 A.D. (the same day of the year, it will be noted, as Edward the Confessor consecrated his Abbey at Westminster). The staff of St. Sophia consisted of sixty priests, a hundred deacons, forty deaconesses, ninety subdeacons, a hundred and ten lectors and twenty-five singers. The size of the building with the amount of staff necessitated new hymns to cover entrances, exits and processions. One of such new hymns was the ὁ μονογενης υιος ("O thou, the only begotten son") used by the Orthodox in the liturgy. The Cherubic Hymn still sung by the Orthodox at the Great Entrance was also sung in Justinian's church in 574.[6]

The rigid attitude of the monastic communities which condemned the use of music was overcome by the efforts of the Emperor and the high ranks of the clergy, who wanted to adorn the divine office with all the splendour which architecture, the arts, music and poetry could provide. The ascendancy of this point of view can be seen from Paul the Silentiary's poetical description of St. Sophia. The poet describes in ornate language every part of the interior and finally the Northex, where the singers chant the psalms:

> "Here, through the night, without a break,
>   springs up a melodious chant,
>   pleasing to the ears of the life-giving Christ,
>   where the precious rites of David the God-fearing
>   are sung in alternating strains
>   by the initiates of David the gentleminded."[7]

Here is the meeting point of hymns and psalms of Jew and Gentile. In these sentences is breathed the life-blood of Christian song—the heritage of the Jew, the Psalms of David (but spoken of with all the feeling of Greek song) of the desire for the beautiful and of Platonic grace—sung neither by Jew nor Greek, but sung in the new air of a new world. New Rome with the Byzantine civilisation made a new synthesis in worship.

THE PSALMS

This brings us back to the first of the Pauline music trinity, psalms. Dr. Egon Wellesz has adequately proved that the method of chanting came from Jewish synagogue use. The performance, of course, varied with the nature of the congregation.[8]

If we expect the Christians of Jewish origin to go on singing what they have always sung in the way they have always sung, we shall not be far wrong about the foundation of Christian psalmody. We may expect and find favourite interpretations which were new. This had been happening for a long time. We may take for example Psalm 110, "The Lord said unto my Lord: sit". Dr. Wilfred Knox points out that "there seems no reason to doubt the possibility that what was originally court-poetry became by interpretation or interpolation, Messianic Psalmody." (The impetus may have come from Persian religion.) "But whatever the origin may have been, (Messianic) hopes of this kind had appeared in different parts of the world whenever intolerable conditions led men to hope for a miraculous deliverance or when it seemed politic to regard the sudden emergence of a new ruler as the realisation of the best hopes of the past."[9]

When our Lord is said to have quoted this psalm in the Temple in the week of his Passion, we are told "the common people heard him gladly" (Mark 12. 37). We may infer from this that the common people could easily understand the interpretation of this psalm in this context. The psalm was already a "Nationale" or a "Komborera Africa". So Peter has no difficulty in using it again as the motley crowd assembles on the day of Pentecost (Acts 2. 34). The writer of Hebrews knows it is a trump card and plays it in his first chapter. (It is doubtful if the crowds who gather for midnight mass at Christmas and hear it read as the epistle really know what is happening.) St. Paul seems to allude to it in Romans 8. 34 and 1 Corinthians 15. 25. The author of Ephesians, like that of Hebrews, puts it in his first chapter (v. 20).

Many further examples could be given. Our point here is that the psalms were domesticated. They were part of the vocabulary of the working classes. The early Christians

quoted Psalms more than any other part of the Old
Testament Canon.

In the ordinary household the family would be used to
some act of piety between work finishing and sundown.
Psalm 145 was in regular use at this time, "Every day will I
give thanks unto thee", and no doubt the stomach called for
the main evening meal to the words of

"The eyes of all wait upon thee, O Lord:
    and thou givest them their meat in due season."

Another for this time was 104. Anybody who has been to
Africa knows how "all beasts of the field drink thereof"
around the waterholes of the bush as the sun goes down.
While the moon is "appointed for certain seasons", the sun
"knoweth his going down".

"The lions roaring after their prey:
    do seek their meat from God."

The very stillness and the frightening sounds of the open
country at night re-echo through this psalm. Meanwhile,
man's wife has gone to prepare "food out of the earth", and
perhaps "wine that maketh glad the heart of man" and oil
(and water) "to make him a cheerful countenance" and
"bread to strengthen man's heart". Before going to bed he
might say Psalm 3:

"I laid me down and slept, and rose up again:
    for the Lord sustained me"

and, bearing in mind there was no public police force,
Psalm 91:

"Thou shalt not be afraid for any terror by night".

4

He wanted to rest under the shadow of the Almighty. If he was married he might dedicate his family life with Psalm 128:

"Thy wife shall be as the fruitful vine".

Enough then to show what Peter and James and John and Paul would have expected from the Psalter. Dr. J. A. Lamb shows that whole psalms were used in much the same way as a modern hymn book. Lamb brings to light an interesting quotation from the apocryphal Apocalypse of Paul which is part of a vision of Paradise.[10]

" 'And as it is done in the heavens, so likewise is it below: for without David it is not lawful to offer a sacrifice unto God; but it must needs be that David sing praises at the hour of the offering of the body and blood of Christ: as it is performed in heaven, so also is it upon earth.' The visionary then asks, 'What is Alleluia?' And in the explanation it is suggested that all present when an Alleluia is sung ought to join in it—'If any sing Alleluia and they that are present sing not with him, they commit sin in that they sing not with him.' The qualification is made that 'he that is able and singeth not' is 'a despiser of the word'.

"There are interesting points here. The singing of psalms is regarded as essential in the Eucharist, that is, supposing that the name David is used for the Psalter, which is the probable interpretation. Further, all who are able to do so—the doting and the aged, for example, are mentioned as excusable—ought to join in the singing. It does seem that the writer is seeking to emphasize the value of psalm-singing in worship and especially in the Eucharist."

Psalm singing as opposed to recitation seems quite the normal use. Note that the Council of Laodicea in its Canon XVII decreed that psalms were not to be sung immediately one after another, but lessons were to be read between. To say the least this is only common decency to the true character of a psalm, a common politeness and care that the

Church chose to neglect in response to the monastic fervour for much time keeping. If it be maintained that the singing of the *Gloria* between psalms satisfies the Canon of Laodicea, then it satisfies the letter but is completely contrary to the spirit of that Canon.[11]

Athanasius and Cassian use Psalm 63:

> "O God, thou art my God:
> early will I seek thee"

in the morning. Chrysostom says the Fathers of the Church appointed it to be used every morning. There is plenty of evidence, including Hilary, to show Psalm 141 was used in the evening:[12]

> "let the lifting up of my hands be an evening sacrifice.
> Set a watch, O Lord, before my mouth:
> and keep the door of my lips"

for in the pre-television era folk did gossip in the evening when the toil of day was finished.

Psalms were indeed the very life blood of Jewish and early Christian piety, associated fully with the toil, the town, the seed time and the sex life of the people. They wore no pseudo-ecclesiastical tone colour. They were used in the home, in the synagogue and within the Christian *Ecclesia*. They were the prayers of the working man and his wife. If we today want to recapture the true nature of the office we must begin here.

It may be a long jump from the Jewish nomadic shepherd in the wilderness with a lion, to the simple pious towns-women in Church of an evening with Hilary of Poitiers or to Bonhoeffer in a Nazi prison May 15th 1943. The last wrote "I am reading the psalms daily, as I have done for years. I know them and love them more than any other book of the Bible."

The modern "with it" theologian who despises the formal daily acts of sacrament, office and private prayer, makes his greatest mistake if he sees these as the continuation of out-worn convention. Martin Thornton rightly postulates these very things as the existential acts of the Body of Christ.[13]

Paul Tillich and others consistently stress the importance of the community. The daily office sustains the ontological unity of the divine organism. Because of the secularity of our times, because man is no longer *homo religiosus*, because he has "come of age", because he lives in a world of general aridity, the divine office is more necessary to him than ever before. If we are to reconstruct the office to be the life blood, to be the existential act of the Body of Christ, then it must be simple enough for man to take it, or part of it, home and use it there. If we are to start thinking of an office which man can sing to himself in the evening by the fireside, or the commercial traveller can take to his hotel room, then our first step must be to sing for him in Church when we meet together evening psalms and morning psalms in such a manner that he takes them out of the door with him. They will need to be known by heart (cf. Chapter Ten). They will need to be tunes that are melodic without a harmony. Old forms and old phrases may not indeed fit. As Thornton says, gazing into an evening sky may not today invite wonder and devotion but rather suggest places to visit. Whatever we sing and say in our daily office, I think it serves no glory if it fails to help man to do his office in private.[14]

CHAPTER FIVE

Church and Synagogue

THE DAILY WORD AND THE DAILY FOOD

In our search for the first principles which underlie the music and daily prayer of the Church we must examine more closely the type of daily worship which St. Paul and those first generation Christians may have used. Their situation was not unlike ours in this, that the committed community of the Body of Christ was a small eclectic group: a community within a community. If we are true to ourselves today we are back in this situation, in which every parish is a missionary parish. This was not true when the Book of Common Prayer was edited in the sixteenth and seventeenth centuries.

Dr. Dugmore makes it clear for us in *The Influence of the Synagogue upon the Divine Office* that the early Church was used to praying together *daily* in the more congested and urban areas.[1] It was of course in the larger cities that the first congregations took root. The beginnings of Christian liturgy and Christian liturgical practice can be seen in contemporary Jewish custom. The Temple had had daily worship for centuries. The institution of the *Ma'amad* linked the village synagogue with the daily Temple worship. (A group of men gathered together for prayer in the village at the precise hour in which the priest offered the sacrifice in the Temple at Jerusalem.)

We are not surprised then to find the Apostolic Tradition, ascribed to Hippolytus (c. 230 A.D.), telling us (xxxv. 1. 2) that faithful men and women will get up at dawn, wash, and pray and "If there should be an instruction in the Word let each one prefer to go thither . . . " and mentioning (xxxvi. 1) "If there is a day when there is no instruction . . . " Our tradition coming from the practice of the synagogue rather than the Temple, we shall notice that the stress is on the word rather than the sacrament of the altar.

"Tell me," says Origen (185/6–253 A.D.) "you who only on festivals come together at Church, are not the other days festal, are they not days of the Lord? . . . Christians eat the flesh of the Lamb on every day, that is they *daily* partake of the flesh of the *Word* of God." And again, "You shall come daily to the wells of the scriptures . . . "[2]

Again, Cyprian (c. 200–258 A.D.) is astonishingly modern as he has to do with the man who says "I'm all right Jack, I keep my religion to myself". "Before all things the Teacher of peace, the Master of unity would not have prayer to be made singly or individually." He goes on to quote our Lord giving a command to pray to Our Father not My Father. How very strange Cyprian would find it as today's Anglican clergy enter one by one into their parish churches of a morning to say "Our Father" to themselves, or with their brethren "in the spirit" not "in the flesh". Augustine tells us that his own mother kept the morning and evening hour of prayer in church every day. One can go on demonstrating the continuing habit of the Church to meet and pray daily. The document known as *The Testament of the Lord* (Asia Minor or Syrian c. 350 A.D.) gives "A Hymn of Praise for the Dawn" with the rubric "at early dawn let the bishop assemble the people . . . "

It has never been the custom in the East to offer the eucharist daily. In the West, Cyprian is found discussing the merits of a morning or evening celebration and suggests "We celebrate the resurrection of the Lord in the morning". The implication is that the practice was a new one, and discussion of this sort was fashionable. A century later the custom was a common one and has survived. It is however to be noted that the custom is not primitive.[3] It has survived particularly where literacy and education were wanting. Within the post-Reformation period in the Church of England the people were able to be fed daily upon "the flesh of the Word of God". Within the present sterile pattern of the daily office, as we practice it in England in the twentieth century, there is no flesh for the stomachs of simple working folk. The ever-growing practice of the daily eucharist is thus not to be attributed to the desire for quasi Roman Catholic practices, but to the desire to give and receive the flesh of the Lord. Dry bones do not nourish. An office with no song, no community, no variation is dry bones. The eucharist does offer the daily and varied "intention", the lights and shades of the calendar (black and red) and the mutual sense of participation which the Anglican communicant so readily appreciates. Martin Thornton comes to the "curious conclusion" that "the Daily Office, recollection and *monthly* communion, forms a more constructive pattern of Christian life than our ideal of frequent communion, much formal devotion, and a comparative disregard of the Office."[4]

The story of the building up of the monastic hours of prayer has been shown to be a Christian deviation, not vitally part of the main stream of parochial devotional expression, but a by-product of asceticism. It was wisely put aside by the reformers. The modern liturgical reformers of the daily office can see much more clearly now than Cranmer could what the layman may hope to enjoy in the daily office. The monastic hours were the product of a process of withdrawal from the world: they were the perquisite of the few. "The synagogue arose out of the need to bring religion to the masses."[5]

THE AUTHORITY OF SCRIPTURE

An important minority within the Anglican Communion

is always pressing the point that the reformation settlement was made upon the principle of scriptural authority. Article VI, for instance, states: "Holy Scripture containeth all things necessary to salvation: so that whatsoever is not read therein, nor may be proved thereby, is not to be required of any man, that it should be believed as an article of the Faith, or be thought requisite or necessary to salvation." They insist that all Prayer Book revisions be strictly scriptural.

Now we are engaged today in Prayer Book revision at home. We are also engaged in seeing what contribution the Church of England can make to ecumenical needs and the progress of the Church entire. Let us be careful to offer as our contribution the spirit of this article as of value to the whole Church. Let us also be careful that it is heeded in our revision. But if we do this we need to be no less careful to see that our manner and intention in the *opus Dei* is after the manner and intention of the *opus Dei* as we find it sprouting in the Acts and the Epistles.

At Beroea in the synagogue they were "studying the scriptures every day" being more "liberal-minded" (Acts 17. 11 N.E.B.). It was not customary to have lections at the daily services in the Jewish synagogue. The Church also began without lections, but by the time of Chrysostom the people were dissatisfied if they left without a daily sermon. "What do I come in for, you say, if I do not hear someone discoursing?" The modern Anglican evensonger says just this. Evensong without a sermon is no evensong: "Better I'd stayed at home!" We know that Ambrose, amongst others of his time, preached daily. Augustine can preach on the Lord's Prayer and say that "Give us this day our daily bread" cannot refer simply to ordinary food, for good and bad receive this food anyway. "What then is the bread? And why is it called daily? . . . There is a daily bread for which the children pray. That is the *Word of God* which is dealt out to us day by day."[6] We shall have to discuss later on, how in our times this word of God is to be dealt in the twentieth century. Enough to notice here that the daily strength of the Christian soul is the daily office. The daily office is the word of God. To be crude, the Holy eucharist is the cake which the children look forward to. The bread is the daily sustenance without which cake gives indigestion.

The bread was not like our daily office, dry bread. "Thou chantest these things every day," says Chrysostom on Psalm 6.[7] The daily singing of solo psalms with responsive endings by all was enjoyed as a common act of faith and hope. In the *Confessions* Augustine says "How I did weep in the hymns and canticles, being moved by the voices of Thy sweet-sounding Church . . . "[8] Augustine was to have the joy, not only of the humble village-style solo psalm singer of early times, but the greater joy of the new style antiphonal psalm chorus developed by Ambrose in Milan—a style which quickly became the norm of the Church, as the Church began its unhappy path under the wing of asceticism towards a formalised dead letter psalmody "in course". (See further Chapter Six.)

Note then that the Jewish form can still be discerned. Augustine follows Cyprian and Tertullian and urges that prayer should begin with "praise". (It was recently, in February 1966, declared in the Church Assembly in London by an unfortunate lay member that to begin the daily office with an act of penitence to the Lord was a "doctrine of the Church". Quite the contrary, it was an unhappy innovation followed in 1552. Psychologically it is quite off the mark.) Only the majesty of God found in prayer, or put into the mind by song, can induce the nature of the creature towards his creator. Otto deals with this in *The Idea of the Holy*: "These feelings (creature feelings) can only arise in the mind as accompanying emotions when the category of 'the numinous' is called into play."[9] George Herbert can tell his congregation at Bemerton just the opposite " . . . until they had begged, obtained pardon for their sins, they were neither able nor worthy to offer their praise to God".[10] One suspects this as being pious comment by a loyal Churchman on a bad liturgy.

To end then with the conclusion of Dr. Dugmore, in the primitive Church: "The pro-Anaphora alone formed the normal service everywhere on weekdays . . . There can be no doubt that public worship at dawn and at sunset was the primitive tradition of the early church. The influence of the synagogue is to be seen in the times of service and the type of service."[11] Dr. Chase has shown that the Lord's Prayer itself is in the spotlight of contemporary worship, and when Paul speaks powerfully and triumphantly in 1 Corinthians 15 of death, when "we shall all be changed in a flash, in the twinkling of an eye" (N.E.B.), he is only putting down involuntarily his faith which he learnt from the '*Amidah*' which he had said every day since he was a little boy.[12] Was it his father, or his mother, who taught him his daily office? Because he had learnt it by heart he could use it to build his life or demonstrate his belief. This is the importance of liturgy. The word of God is the strength of man. We shall have more to say of the need for repetition and the use of memory in the daily office, to make it effective, in chapter ten.

THE SYNAGOGUE AND THE PARISH CHURCH

There is little left in early Christian psalmody from the traditions of the Jewish high feasts. On the whole the legacy is the legacy of the synagogue and of the home rather than of the Temple and national high days. Theologically this is accounted for by the desire of the Gentile and Pauline Christianity to get away from the emphasis on collective salvation and replace it by the emphasis on the individual hope in Christ.[13] There is some trace of lections and prayers continuing from the great feasts, but little of psalmody. We may conjecture that if a central high altar had been built for Christians in Jerusalem under a different political situation the inheritance of psalmody would have been otherwise.

We may find some food for thought here on the liturgical relationships between cathedral and parish church. "The attitude of the Temple was theocentric and ritualistic, that of the synagogue anthropocentric and democratic . . . The synagogue was a house of prayer, meditation, and most important, study."[14] We read few pages of the New Testament without breathing in this atmosphere of "teach-in". We may be misled in our general attitude towards the liturgy of the Temple in Jerusalem from the references to theological dialogue. One has in mind, for instance, Luke 2. 46 when Jesus was in the Temple "sitting in the midst of the doctors, both hearing them, and asking them questions", or again John 10. 23, 24 "and Jesus walked in the temple . . . Then came the Jews round about him, and said unto him . . . " These things took place in "Solomon's porch" or the Hall of Solomon. This building linked the life of the Temple with the ordinary country synagogue, a place for meetings, discussion and study. Its relationship with the Temple was such as the relationship between the Chapel of Unity at Coventry with the cathedral itself. We do well to try and get a balanced perspective here and not to confuse these somewhat specialised activities of the Hall of Solomon with the daily musical activities in the routine worship which engaged the population as a whole and about which we hear so little in the course of the gospel story.

THE TENSION OF TRANSITION

In evaluating the uses of the Psalter in the early Church we must remember there is a double tension. Following the destruction of Jerusalem there was the natural desire to hold on to tradition within the synagogue, whilst Christians had the added tension of liberalised interpretations. For example the Hosanna in Psalm 118 was a cry for help: the Christians soon made it a shout of jubilation.

Professor Eric Werner draws out the pattern of the psalms in the early Church, and goes on: "Most of these psalms also form an integral part of the Synagogue ritual."[15] Thus Church and Synagogue use Psalm 100, the *Jubilate*, as a morning hymn. Both use Psalms 91 and 134 for the evening. The synagogue sabbath use of Psalm 34:

> "I will alway give thanks . . .
> Come, ye children . . .
> I will teach you"

gets the added Christian motif on the Sunday Agape of

> "O taste, and see".

But the little despised groups found new and comforting food in Psalm 133:

> "Behold, how good and joyful a thing it is:
> brethren, to dwell together in unity!"[16]

Again Eusebius tells us that they took Psalm 92 from the synagogue and hallowed it on Sunday:

> "It is a good thing to give thanks . . .
> And to sing . . .
> Such as are planted in the house of the Lord."[17]

What wealth and beauty and unity of prayer there is here which has all been overthrown for us Anglicans in our present use. One must remember that the medieval Church endeavoured unsuccessfully to keep both the secular, synagogue psalmody and also the monastic, ascetic psalmody "in course". With the exception of *Venite*, Cranmer only

passed to us the latter. I shall develop this further in chapter
six.

As the Church—the people of the "way"—grew, so the
Jewish zeal to outlaw it and banish it from the face of the
earth became stronger. Because of this antagonism, together
with the Jewish/Gentile controversy inside the Church, we
hear gradually less and less of psalmody and more and more
of hymns until after Nicaea.[18] Then, with the secularisation
of Christianity, the Jewish Christians were crushed between
the Gentile Church and the Synagogue and tended to fall
within one or other wholly. Thus after Nicaea specifically
Christian interpretations and customs take over. "Ten
strings are known of the psaltery and ten commandments of
the Law. To sing and to chant (*psaltere*) is usually an occupa-
tion of loving men. The old man is in fear, the new one is in
love. Thus we discern two Testaments . . . "[19] Augustine is
mild where Chrysostom, further to the East, where Jewish
culture was more entrenched, was still constantly thundering
against his Jewish opposition.

Following Jewish custom, women are encouraged not to
sing for "the voice of woman leads to licentiousness".
Choruses of women's voices were not unknown, but the
mixture of voices was considered a danger to the harmony of
sound and mind, though Ambrose thought women could
sing a psalm well.[20] To this day the Church still has a pre-
disposition towards the male voice choir; though the true
reason is seldom stated, it remains a part of the subconscious
raison d'être.

Again, instrumental accompaniments were officially
outlawed after the fall of Jerusalem, as a sign of mourning
for the loss of the Temple worship. Compare Isaiah 24. 8:

> "The mirth of tabrets ceaseth . . .
> The joy of the harp ceaseth . . . "

But it seems the conflict with Hellenism and the influence

of Roman syncretistic cults with their doubtful rites and orgies with cymbal, string and flute had already put the mind of the Synagogue against instrumental accompaniment to worship. When Aquinas says "Our Church does not admit instruments . . . lest it seem to Judaize", he is in fact a thousand years behind the times![21] The Hebrew psalms required a lot of brass, but the instruments had long since been put away.

In the western gentile Church, what has become known as the Ambrosian antiphonal psalmody became the norm. In the Armenian rites we find much more of the early Jewish solo and responsive psalmody, as indeed had been the custom of the synagogue. There is research waiting to be done into the primitive Jewish origins of much Armenian practice.

Generally speaking the Temple authority was antagonistic to sectarianism and so by implication to Jesus and "the way". In the early centuries the Christian heritage of worship was drawn almost entirely from the synagogue and furthermore "Psalmody was the greatest legacy of the Synagogue to Jewish Christianity, and thence to the Gentile Church".[22]

CHAPTER SIX

Cranmer and the Reform

AFTER THE PRIMITIVE HARE

The big rush to be primitive is rather outdated. Nevertheless let us observe that Cranmer writes in the Book of Common Prayer: "and furthermore notwithstanding that the ancient Fathers have divided the Psalms into seven portions, whereof every one was called a nocturn; now of late time, a few of them have been daily said and the rest utterly omitted."[1] Gregory Dix comments on this: "The unbroken recitation of the whole Psalter straight through, instead of the daily recitation of certain fixed and selected Psalms as had been the Jewish and pre-Nicene custom of private prayer, was a monastic innovation of the Fourth Century, which Cranmer supposes primitive."[2] What is important, is that the Book of Common Prayer with its numerically ordered monthly recitation is a modification of the monastic use of the Psalter, and not in any way a representation of "primitive secular use"; the proper psalms possibly excepted.

It was said earlier that "We suffer from uncompleted Cranmer". The Book of Common Prayer was intended to heal the gap between layman and cleric. The Book is supposed to bridge the gap between the primer and the breviary. Where the psalms are concerned it has not done it very well. Cranmer did not go back far enough.

W. C. Bishop says we see in Tertullian (*Apol.* 39) the

beginning of Western secular vespers, as opposed to Roman medieval Vespers, which nearly everywhere superseded the former when the flood of monastic innovation of the fourth century swept over the Church.[3] The service originally was one of casual psalm singing, probably often solo, no lessons, ending with a bishop's prayer. The shadow of this remains in the Mozarabic service of vespers. A parallel service for mornings, the heart of which was psalms 148 to 150, survived in medieval times. We may note that even as late as Athanasius or Augustine, it was known for the bishop or precentor to "pitch" upon a psalm at will during a service, and have it sung. (See St. Augustine on Psalm 138.)[4]

At the Holy Eucharist it is the gradual which occupies most psalm interest in the primitive Church. In fact it was so important that a good gradual singer could consequently be elevated to the episcopate.[5] Duchesne maintains that the gradual had an intrinsic value in the service, whilst the introit, offertory and communion psalms were introduced "merely to occupy attention during long ceremonies".[6] It was ordered in Egypt that psalms should be read as long as people were filing into church. "We may gather from Theodore of Mopsuestia and Narsai that the Offertory had been done in solemn silence, but then for Augustine the Offertory and Communion Psalmody is an African innovation, and he writes a pamphlet to defend it.[7] Dr. G. G. Willis has shown in *St. Augustine's Lectionary* that the gradual psalm was appointed side by side with the epistle and gospel; for example:

1 Timothy 1. 15   "Jesus came into the world to save sinners"

Psalm 95. 6   "O come, let us worship and fall down"

Luke 17. 15   "And one of them, when he saw that he was healed, turned back . . . and fell down on his face at his feet"[8]

But as time goes on, as people's oblations become rare and lay communions less frequent, the offertory and communion psalms become first a selection of verses, and then disappear. By the eleventh century only two or three verses survive in Roman choir books for the communion psalm, whilst the offertory psalm, except at requiems, survived only in the antiphon. Now this is the anthem of the Book of Common Prayer, which is finally degraded to a "sentence" —"said". Such an uncomely part of the liturgy.

Much of this early psalmody seems to have been solo or responsorial, but we find that great bursts of music were common to Chrysostom and Hilary (Ps. 65). "Let him that stands outside the Church hear the voice of the people praying, let him perceive the glorious sound of our hymns and hear the responses—the offices of the Divine Sacraments . . . Let us fight against the devil and his weapons with the *sound* of our prayer, and let the victory of our war be proclaimed with the *voice* of exultation."[9] There is no modern Anglican anaemia about this. Jerome can write to his dear Paula, "The labourer, while he holds the handle of the plough sings Alleluia: the tired reaper employs himself in the psalms; and the vine dresser, while lopping the vines with his curved hook sings something of David. These are our ballads in this part of the world: these, to use a common expression, are our love songs."[10]

Prior to the monastic domination of the liturgy, the laity enjoyed a simple office of song and a Holy Eucharist with a gradual and "background psalmody" selected to taste. Psalmody "in course" was a monastic product.

THE MEDIEVAL PSALTER

As churchmen, we must venerate the Gregorian Psalter which carried the *opus Dei* through the Medieval Age in the West. Lauds had a carefully selected psalm for each day, Psalm 92 for the Sabbath, "Such as are planted in the house of the Lord"; Psalm 93 for the day of Resurrection, "The Lord is King . . . holiness becometh thine house for ever"; Psalm 5, the "Lead me, O Lord", for the beauty of a Monday morning. Compline had that beautiful daily fixed combination 4, 31, 91 and 134, which today so attracts any young Anglicans who once get hold of it. For the rest, the psalms were sung "in course" in one week. The length and dullness of this practice lent itself to the abuse of substituting shorter Saint's Days psalms for ferials. The so-called Devotions of the Blessed Sacrament on Thursdays and of St. Mary on Saturdays also helped to ease the burden. Thus we reach Cranmer's dictum "There was never any thing by the wit of man so well devised, or so sure established, which in continuance of time hath not been corrupted".[11] We find intermingled with the beauty of the chosen psalmody of the Gregorian Psalter such nonsense as the three nocturnes "in course" being associated with the Patriarchial, Legal and Christian Ages, and Psalm 1 with Abel, Psalm 2 with Cain and similar enormities.[12]

Now what of the other systems of psalmody? Quignon's simplifications (1535) wisely gave mattins the greatest share of the burden.[13] There was some reference to betrayal and crucifixion on Wednesdays and Fridays. The monotony of high and holy days such as Christmas having no propers made the system unbearable. The Ambrosian and Mozarabic uses have little to offer us today. The Orthodox had their Psalter divided into twenty Cathisimata sung "in course". That road lay wide open to abuse. The later Parisian Breviary which abandoned completely all attempt to keep the numerical order of the psalms makes the most enlightened picture, Sunday being given up to psalms of praise, Thursday to love, Wednesday to hope, etc. . . . Alas, the popularity of this idea meant that soon there were very nearly as many breviaries in France as there were Dioceses!

The monastic domination of the Psalter, and the method of singing it "in course", was one of the contributary causes towards the hardening of ecclesiastical opinion against the medieval troubadour. These professional musicians did in fact succeed in entering the churches and reinforcing the choir, and giving occasional performances. "But the general and persistent hostility of the church to the troubadours was due to the comparative scarcity of reference to vernacular poetry."[14] What opportunity indeed some of the psalms offered the troubadours' art! The strait-jacket of medieval psalmody, Latin "in course", kept them out. As then, so it is now.

CHAPTER SEVEN

Aspects of the Office in the Eighteenth Century

ALTAR AND FONT

The eighteenth century begins with the tensions of Calvinism brought in with William of Orange. William's wife, Queen Mary, went to Canterbury Cathedral one morning, and in that same afternoon to a parish church for evensong. "She heard there a very good sermon, but she thought herself in a Dutch Church, for the people stood on the Communion Table to look at her."[1] The eighteenth century ends with the font of Westminster Abbey popped away "topsy turvy" in a side room to make room for a monument.[2] These two perhaps insignificant acts are symbolic of the age. Sermons and political monuments now take the place of the sacraments in the minds of the people. Altar and font are redundant. Pulpits grow bigger and bigger and choirs grow smaller. Church choirs exist to offer praise around the throne of God, the place of the presence. Where there is no presence, no *Shekinah*, the choir ceases to know what it is to do. Man has now taken the place of God in his own house.

Fine sermons, great monuments, reflect the influence of the deistic controversy. All that was mysterious and supernatural must be reduced to what was natural and reasonable. During this century the ordered Anglican mystique of men such as Jeremy Taylor (1613–1667) and Bishop Ken (1637–1711) gave way before the more popular type of worship dominated by hymn singing wisely pioneered by

Isaac Watts (1674–1748),[3] Less responsible men than Watts found there was no need to bother with the body of Christ. Deistic and Unitarian theology, such as Matthew Tindal's *Christianity as old as the Creation* (1730), sold well.[4] Men were tired of the religious feuds of the previous century which had brought Church and state to chaos. Men were tired of war with France, and the new St. Paul's in London with its secular look was a mark of the new age. Bishop Compton had called upon England to see it as a great thanksgiving for peace. His visitation articles for his fine new cathedral required the Dean to provide for the mind of the laity, by providing sermons on all feasts and fasts of the Church. He also attempted to make the cathedral staff a praying body, himself constantly being celebrant at the altar and insisting that all in holy orders make their communion together *every* Sunday "unless hindered by some lawful cause to be approved by the Dean and Chapter". His successors showed less concern for Anglican piety, less enthusiasm for the spread of the gospel beyond the sea, and gave less time to finding priests to serve in India and America.[5] The Church was weary, but it was also rich in high places—Blenheim Palace for the Duke of Marlborough, who had saved England, and great ecclesiastical palaces for those lords spiritual who were not unlike the Vicar of Bray.

COMMUNITY AND COMMON PRAYER

The Dean of Westminster found it difficult to stop butchers carrying meat through the Abbey during services. Boys of the school carved their names on the Coronation Chair, and at least two choristers were drowned in the Thames. It was an age of indiscipline and laxity. The family around this great Church and others like it was breaking up.[6] Abbot and monk had made way for Dean and choristers. Deans now gave less care to the little boys, it was ceasing to be *us* at our prayers. The mystical unity in the sacraments was gone. Choirs never stayed beyond the Prayer for the Church. The *Sanctus* was sung as an introit. Of fourteen service settings printed in Boyce's *Cathedral Music* between 1760–1778 only one (Tallis) was printed with *Gloria in Excelsis*.[7] Things were better at Durham. Thomas Ebdon (1738–1816) wrote a service setting for that cathedral, which was remarkable for that period in having a full sung communion. Durham had reintroduced a weekly communion in 1685.[8]

Some would have liked to see the great Abbey Church at Westminster alive with monks. King Henry expected it to be alive with boys, priests and old soldiers. The almsman "decayed in the King's Service" was expected to be part of the daily praying community and later were allowed "a penny-a-piece . . . towards his offering at Mass". The canons, if in London, were all expected to be at mattins, mass and evensong daily. At festivals four of the old soldiers and four of the clerks were to make their communions with *all* the members of the chapter.

The choristers were to be part of (not apart from) the primary educational foundation. In King Henry's day one might have expected to see at service time:

> 1 dean
> 12 canons of the chapter
> 12 minor canons
> 12 lay singing men
> 10 choristers
> 2 sextons
> 1 schoolmaster
> 39 scholars
> 12 old soldiers

saying their prayers, one hundred and one joining together in the corporate daily office of this great house.

One of the last glimmers of this former glory came on

June 3rd 1760. Dean Zachary Pearce gathered up his flock to celebrate the bicentenary of Queen Elizabeth's charter. "The whole Company sat down to a Dinner in the Hall, the Dean, Prebendaries, and upper officers of the Church being at the Upper End of the Hall; the Minor Canons, Gentlemen of the Choir, Singing Boys and inferior servants of the Church on the Eastern side of it, the King's Scholars on the West side, and the Almsmen at a table placed in the middle." Some family! At 4.30 they went back into the choir for evensong.[9]

Today we attempt to recover the theology of a community "doing" the eucharist together. It was at this time that the worshipping community broke down. This is why Martin Thornton is so absolutely to the point in his *English Spirituality* when he pleads that it is a waste of time planning the Prayer Book for the eclectic Sunday congregation.[10] The worship of the Church of England is the worship of a community. The Prayer Book is deeply rooted in the Benedictine Abbey, it cannot fit comfortably into a Sunday Special. The Archbishop of Canterbury said at Nashdom on July 15th 1965, "and so it is that the Benedictine Way really underlies the Book of Common Prayer, where the same trinity of liturgy, office and personal prayer is found for the joy of us all."[11] In an earlier age, the converting power of St. Augustine's monks had not been their sermons, but their community life. The eighteenth century now takes the choral office away from the sacraments, away from the community, and exhibits it as a musical experience. A contemporary, Thomas Brown, complained that the choir of Westminster came "reaking hot from the baudy-house into the Church—and hick-up over a little of the litany". The "Singing Church" was to sink still lower.[12]

The bubbling spirits and colourful gaiety of the Restoration had caused the country squires to put in the churches the royal coat of arms. The divines, in similar mood, had added the state prayers (following the Scottish Book of

1637) as an appendage to the daily office. It was a momentary ecstasy, which was natural for a year or two, but which has been a misplaced article of luggage to be carried along daily by the faithful ever since (cf. page 140). The seventeenth century gave us also the theology of the "divine right of kings" which caused Lancelot Andrewes such anguish.[13] So following on, the eighteenth century gave us from its greatest Church composer, Dr. Boyce, "Give the King thy judgements". It also gave the congregation before the sermon the poor rate assessment and the notices about window tax.[14] The Bishop of Carlisle could conveniently put down an insurrection. The ecclesiastical convocations became unnecessary. Everybody was too well involved already in the party political machinery.[15] The Government was later (1818) to be able to allot public money to build churches in areas of national industrialisation, in the hope of dealing with national moral degeneration. It needed Wesley to tell them that it could only be done with humble prayers and praises. There being no community of worship, Wesley was to recreate a new community in spirit to be developed later into the separate community of Methodists.

Many reasons might be given for the original causes of the separation, and the fracture of the Church into denominationalism. Certainly one cause was the failure of the Book of Common Prayer, as printed, to hold together the Church as a body. It had ceased to be a true expression of contemporary experience. The people had moved to a new age. The Book had gone stale and no longer fed the people. The people had left the table and so the family was almost extinct.

A TIME FOR REFORM

In St. Paul's at the great anniversary service of the Sons of the Clergy, sober churchmen saw with disgust a careless, pleasure-loving audience listening to singers promiscuously gathered from the theatres, and laughing, eating and drinking their wine in the intervals. At Gloucester, a lady who thought her deceased daughter had become a robin was allowed by the Dean to have an aviary near the high altar. During services, which tended to be too long, liveried servants could enter a family pew with sherry and light refreshments at an appropriate interval.[16]

The Three Choirs Festival, was being held at Worcester, Gloucester and Hereford. During its course Dr. Thomas Bisse preached, on September 7th 1720. He preached unheeded for reform. He told his vast musical congregation that in the days of King Edward VI mattins was not spoilt with long intercessions, and litanies had their proper time and occasion. The service, he said, ended with three collects, then an anthem, Prayer of Chrysostom and the Grace. The service "ought to consist chiefly of praises, thanksgivings, manifested in doxologies and hallelujahs, psalms, hymns and anthems". He reminded his contemporaries that music brought Augustine of Hippo to his conversion; he recalled them to the part the laity had in the ordered worship; and that before the Prayer Book was printed, versicles and responses were divided between priest and choir and not as now, priest and answer. Dr. Bisse could see that the song was going from the churches. The voice of Dr. Bisse was not the voice of the time.[17]

THE BISHOPS' CALL

A man like Ralph Thoresby writes in his diary, "I shall never, I hope, so long as I am able to walk, forbear a constant attendance upon the public common prayer twice everyday, in which course I have found much comfort". Though the body corporate in worship was growing smaller, in the eighteenth century the daily offices were still a reality for a great number of the faithful laity. Cranmer's book undoubtedly had worked as he intended it to work. In 1669 the Archdeacon of Durham instructed his curate at Easington to say the daily office on working days at "six in the morning and six in the evening, as the most convenient for labourers and business men". Good Bishop Turner of Ely could charge his diocese in 1686—"I could almost kneel" to ask clergy with one or two gentry or school children to say "in Church" the daily office. Within a year or two Bishop Ken of Bath and Wells makes the same plea to "offer it up in Church" or, if this is not possible, then "in your family at least". Bishop Patrick of Ely tells his clergy in 1692 to say the daily office with their families if there is no congregation. A Mrs. Thornton had the offices said daily in her house. Granville said his with his servant when travelling and George Herbert expected those not in for the daily office to pause at work. William Law, founding a school in the village of Kings Cliffe in Northamptonshire, insists that children attend divine service "as well on weekdays as on Sundays".[18]

Chrysostom (345–407 A.D.) had had to appeal to Psalm 134 v. 2, "Ye that by night stand in the house of the Lord", to get his people to attend the daily office. Jungmann tells us Ambrose and Augustine had congregations at the daily office before there was a daily eucharist.[19] St. Hilary's congregation assembled day by day. The Council of Toledo 633 called for a unified morning hour for all. Bishop Turner in 1686 was not asking the laity to do anything new. In fact somebody one day needs to explain to us why people loved the Coverdale version of the psalms so much that they refused to sing them to the words of the new English Bible of 1611. Had they really learnt them on Sundays? There had been a considerable use of the daily Psalter among the laity which unfortunately disappeared during the eighteenth century.[20]

Patterson's account of the London churches shows that in 1714 a large proportion were open daily for morning and evening prayer, but he says it was visibly falling off and in some places evening prayer was discontinued. Morning bell was usually at 6 a.m. Archbishop Sancroft in a circular letter to the bishops of his province had, in 1688, found it necessary to urge the public performance of the daily office "in all market and other towns". That the Puritan Baxter could say "it must needs be a sinful impediment against other duties to say Common Prayer twice a day", demonstrates well enough that it was a well followed practice. It was dying now; not because of the Puritans.[21]

A HYMN TO HELP

Music had been taken from prayer. People were bored by endless recitation and one by one lapsed away. In the place of liturgy they developed the modern version of the hymn. Begun as a substitute for psalm it develops in form into endless verse after verse. The utter triteness of so much of this is, in no small measure, responsible for our present decadence in worship as a nation. Superficially it may look as if the hymn is the one feature in modern Anglican worship which is popular in the pew. Nevertheless, its unintelligent use and the often puerile form of both the written word and song, has contributed in no small measure to the collapse, in general, of public worship.

What concerns us in eighteenth century practice is that Isaac Watts can say in his preface (1707) "When we are just entering into an Evangelic Frame . . . the Clerk parcels out to us . . . something . . . extremely Jewish and cloudy, that darkens our sight of God our Saviour". This was invariably read in a dead manner, for Watts also says "the congregation of choristers in Cathedral Churches are the only Levites that *sing* praise unto the Lord with the word of David and Asaph the seer". No better comment on the contention in the earlier parts of this study could be made. Psalms, if not sung, erode.[22]

The English liturgy had spoken to the Elizabethans in

terms of their own environment and needs of the day. It lapped their everyday existence. A. L. Rowse in *The England of Elizabeth* can say "It is impossible to overestimate the influence of the Church's routine of prayer and good works upon society: the effect upon imagination and conduct of the liturgy with its piercing and affecting phrases . . . " Now society had changed. The liturgy was still Elizabethan and no longer gave "satisfaction to the innermost impulses of the heart".[23]

A different method of solving the problem was advanced by John Stephens (1702), a lawyer who took holy orders. He complained that the morning service had become "mourning service". He tried and failed to get authority to move and so, as it were, went underground. The holy group he formed had as a rule of life "to meet daily at five in the morning, at a daily communion". This was the full service, not the customary ante-communion which he terms an "abominable abuse". However, John Stephens was no more able to alter the laxity of the times with his community than Nicholas Ferrar had been able to do with his at Little Gidding.[24]

THE MUSICIANS' OFFERING

The musicians' answer to this liturgical stupor was to develop the double chant. This has now dominated all public worship in the Church of England for two centuries. The Rev. Luke Flintoft (d. 1727), a minor canon of Westminster, published a collection of chants which included the one popularly known as *Flintoft in G Minor*. (See example page 114.) The formal singing in big churches of long helpings of daily psalmody must have been much eased for the choirs by the jauntiness which the double chant made possible. In 1768 Boyce published in *Cathedral Music* Volume II three double chants and only one single one.

So the new Anglican double chant, together with the

Methodist form of hymn, was to hold together congregations for another two centuries. One could scarcely say they were held together by the ordered liturgical worship of the Book of Common Prayer. This is the kind of thing that bishops say at Lambeth Conferences.[25] Without the hymn, what would have happened to the congregations in the eighteenth century and after? Liturgy was almost dead, and its sick and languishing frame was to be nourished from without by the intrusion of endless hymnody.

"AND NOW THE MERRY ORGAN"

Another great intrusion into worship at this time was the pipe organ. Organs had been about for a long time. Now they began to be no longer a rather comic little sideline for special days, but something of a secularising monster. The organ became bigger and took its place in all the larger market town type of churches. In 1337, Jean de Grandisson, Bishop of Exeter, had allowed the organ to play on principal double feasts during *Kyrie, Gloria,* Sequence, *Credo,* offertory, *Sanctus, Agnus* and *Deo Gratias.*[26] The Restoration composers had used the instrument quite freely to enhance the "verse" anthem, and to supplement the musical effects of service settings of canticles.

In Queen Anne's time, it was noted that churches without organs had thinner congregations. We need look no further than the contemporary pamphleteer to know that this century was ushered in with a rush of organs. The organ at Tiverton occasioned *The Lawfulness of Instrumental Music in the Holy Offices* from Dodwell. N.N. writes *A Discourse concerning the Rise of Cathedral Worship* published in 1699 and quotes Isidore, Wicliffe and Erasmus against musical instruments in worship.[27]

Now in the eighteenth century the organ becomes a supplement to the liturgy, just as the hymn was. The organ helped the liturgy along on its jaunty way, for with all truth it was as dull as ditchwater for the consumer. In the best places everybody could sit and listen after the psalms to an exhibition of the art of the organ. Sir John Hawkins, writing the introduction to the 1788 edition of Boyce's *Cathedral Music*, can say that sometimes the organist can draw more people than the preacher (and at this period preaching really was followed by a great number, much as League football is followed in the twentieth century). We shall have cause to refer to this question of relative magnetic powers again in the chapter dealing with our own contemporary situation.

Sir John Hawkins also tells us that Robinson in St. Lawrence Jewry would play airs in two or three parts on cornets and noisy stops, whereas Boyce seldom used anything but the quiet and smooth stopped diapason. When Boyce was buried in St. Paul's under the dome, it was said there was "no greater artist" in St. Paul's save Christopher Wren.[28]

At the Abbey in the west of London town the appointment of a new organist shows us too clearly that the judgement of Hawkins was not the typical view of his times, any more than the judgement of Tudway had been of his. The Dean and chapter at Westminster appointed John Robinson in 1727 to be their Master of the Choristers. He succeeded William Croft whose Burial Sentences remain to this day a milestone of beauty, aptly fitting the aim and stratagem of the Book of Common Prayer. In Croft the church still had a link in spirit with the sixteenth-century style of Tallis. With John Robinson comes again the secular blast first felt at the Restoration.

For thirty-five years Robinson was to rule at Westminster. Boyce was kind enough to say that he was "a most excellent performer on the organ". Dr. Jocelyn Perkins can write in the twentieth century that it must have been "banal to the degree . . . calculated to drive out every refined mind from the building with all possible celerity". He was indeed "a harpsichord player, and endeavoured to perform upon the organ, music only fit for the former instrument". This is the wisdom of an Abbey priest in our times. The wisdom of the Abbey priest of the eighteenth century was that Robinson was the style for them. Worship needs to be tickled up, and this is how we do it![29]

Towards the end of his first year at the Abbey, Robinson found himself organising a coronation for George II. Perhaps we should congratulate him for finding room for Handel's anthem *Zadok the Priest* which has become almost a *sine qua non* for coronations ever since. Needless to say the Abbey had to have a bigger and better organ for such an occasion and Mr. Schrider duly built one, but note, "above the altar"! No wonder that the tomb of Edward the Confessor behind the high altar suffered so much. There had been a time when the Abbey itself had been rebuilt by Henry III to be a suitable clothing for the tomb of the patron saint of England. What was prayer now?

The coronation over, what does one do with organs over altars? *The British Journal* of February 10th 1728 says "it has been presented to the said Abbey by his Majesty"; the cost was £1,000. The secular authority, be it noted, Sir Robert Walpole, Prime Minister, gave authority for a new screen at the entrance of the choir. No mean little job, for it was not finished until August 1730. There were some who complained that when you now entered the Abbey all you met was Schrider's organ and case looking at you high up in the centre on its new loft. These however were minority opinions. Most were pleased that they could listen to this three-manualled creation, with its fantastic new device, the swell box. In due course (probably July 11th 1778) were added thirteen independent pedal pipes, open, of wood. It was the first appearance in England, it seems, of great booms from pedals. Another landmark in the rendering of worship in the Abbey Church of Westminster and also in the Church of England![30]

Meanwhile more important things were happening below the organ loft. Henry III's choir fittings were removed by the surveyor Henry Keene and were replaced by what have been termed "sham gothic enormities of oak and cast iron." We are only concerned with this in that a more solid division of the church takes place between the choir and the nave, and the length of the choir seating is reduced. It was no longer necessary to have such a long row of stalls for monk or even prebend.

This destruction of the medieval oak choir in the Abbey ordered by the Dean and chapter on May 6th 1774 was cruel. Nevertheless, was not the reduction of the number of stalls from sixty-four to thirty-four a sadder tale still, in terms of the song of the Church in this fine building? We miss the wood, for we know what is lost! Fewer of us are aware of what was lost in the praises of God.[31]

The time had come, therefore, for organs all over the country to grow bigger, to go up higher. The time had come for human voices to have less to offer and often to take a second place in the Sunday performance of Christian witness. The organist becomes separate from his choir both in physical proximity and also in the offering of worship. He becomes an entity apart from his choir. Thus, the body corporate at prayer disintegrates further.

At the beginning of the century the ordinary town church at its daily office had a congregation but no organ. At the conclusion of the century it had an organ, but no congregation.

CHAPTER EIGHT

Aspects of the Office in the Nineteenth Century

THE SURVIVAL OF A REMNANT

The Lord Bishop of London stood on Ludgate Hill and said to Sir Robert Phillimore: "I look at that great Cathedral and think of its large revenues and great responsibilities and ask myself what good it is doing to this great city, and I feel compelled to answer, not any, to a single soul in it."[1]

Inside, the Cathedral was beginning to get loaded with national effigies behind iron railings (which, together with the railways, were a sign of wealth and the new industrial prosperity). The Abbey was now full up. "A disgusting heap of trash" wrote Sidney Smith in 1819 of the monuments in St. Paul's. Fourteen years earlier, when admitted to a canonry in St. Paul's, he wrote "My sentences are frozen as they come out of my mouth." He was no doubt better clothed for the conditions than the wretched choristers, who were now reduced to the ridiculous number of eight. Behind them sat six professional lay singers, three on each side. This is all that remained of the thirty men who at one time sang as vicars choral for the prebendaries.[2]

Thomas Attwood presided at the organ for forty years. He no doubt gained some joy from spending much of his time in earlier life writing for the stage. Perhaps it is no accident that amongst his most famous anthems are "Come, Holy Ghost, our souls inspire" and "Let the words of my mouth", for indeed there seemed a lacking of the Spirit and

6   81

a surfeit of words from the pulpit. The ordering of worship
in so great a building with such meagre vocal resources must
have been an unenviable lot for so talented a musician. His
little anthem "Teach me O Lord", so often sung by village
choirs today, was the kind of thing with which they could
cope.

The organ made up for the lack of liturgy. One Sunday
afternoon in 1829 Mendelssohn was playing in this Cathedral
after evensong, as he so often loved to do, and was holding
fast the congregation which contemporary liturgy failed to
hold. The vergers, who despaired of trying to usher the
crowds out through the doors, eventually contrived to let
the air out of the bellows in the middle of a Bach fugue!
A bishop's brother-in-law was given the appointment of
precentor in March 1819, only three years after his ordination.
He reigned in charge of the cathedral music for sixty-seven
years! It is said that when he did make one of his occasional
visits to the Cathedral in 1872, he was refused his stall by the
Dean's verger, who did not know him.

Mattins was sung daily at 9.45 and evensong at 3.15.
Quite a different business to the early 6 a.m. service of a
century or two earlier! It was thought, in a strange flutter
of enthusiasm, that some provision should be made for
working people, so a said office was ordered to take place
earlier in a chapel. Needless to say this was left by the
canons to the minor canons. The minor canons in turn hired
out the job to a reader, whom they paid fifty guineas a year
so that they too could stay in bed. Was any further degradation of the daily office possible?[3]

St. Paul's was no worse than other places. An amusing
pamphlet was published in 1851 which supposes a midnight
conversation between Westminster Abbey and the Roman
Catholic church of St. George: (*Westminster speaks*) " . . . yet
as I daily hear the lessons of Holy Writ read and chanted,
by the half sleepy Canons and choir to a wretched congregation, I sicken for the want of earnestness and faith which

seem to have taken their departure from this pampered church . . . " (*St. George's*) " . . . one cannot wonder that you should be tired of their dull and respectable mediocrity . . . the luxurious Dean and Chapter, with plenty of riches and no ecclesiastical power . . . the humdrum choir singing to your bare walls their professional praises . . . "[4]

When the monks' choir of Benedictines was dispersed at Westminster (January 16th 1540), the secular choir allowed after the Dissolution consisted of ten boys, twelve laymen and twelve minor canons. By the early nineteenth century the boys had sunk to eight, the men to ten and the minor canons ceased to sing as a body. Westminster was fortunate to have John Ireland as Dean from 1818 to 1842, a musical man who was keen to bring his choir back to capitular strength. The men of the choir had an unfortunate habit of slipping away during the sermon to sing elsewhere, and when Frederick Bridge took over the organ loft in 1882 he noted that on some occasions all six men from one side had "melted away".

The Reverend John Jebb, a canon residentiary of Hereford, penned a scathing criticism of the Abbey. After writing of "coldness, meagreness and irreverence" he goes on to say the choir was "barely tolerable". The lessons were read as if the clerk was reading in a court of law. "A wretched clock was the signal for beginning to race through the office. The books were torn and soiled and the surplices more black than white . . . The whole of the Church plainly indicated the mechanical performance of a burdensome duty." Nevertheless at the Abbey they seem to have had less of the organ than at St. Paul's, for Mr. Turle (1831–1882) rarely played "in" on weekdays while the playing "out" was restricted to a few chords.[5]

If the canonical daily offices were terrible, there were signs of life elsewhere. Dean Trench instituted at the Abbey in 1858 a popular Sunday night evensong supported by a voluntary choir. Psalms were printed on calico and hung up in the nave; two thousand could be present. Preaching on the first occasion the Dean said, "If you will come here in such numbers as to shut them (the rich) out from the evening service of this Abbey, we should only be better pleased, and should thank God that the purpose for which these services were commenced, namely the preaching of the Gospel to the poor—was in fact being fulfilled."[6]

THE LAYMEN SPEAK OUT

At Winchester Samuel Sebastian Wesley, a brilliant organist (if eccentric personality), was raging at the clergy. The Cathedral Commissioners had discovered that minor canons now did little, and reduced their number. "The clergy," he said, "are supposed to have been better singers . . . The singing of the clergy has been discouraged and is now almost silent." At this point in 1853, with this epic pronouncement of an enthusiastic layman, we reach one of the great signposts of English church music.[7]

Way back before the Dissolution, church music had begun to be false to its origins, to become the work of the professional rather than of the body corporate. In the succeeding centuries we have seen the cathedral statutory body gradually decrease in number and recede in the offering of the daily office. Now after three hundred years the fracture is complete. The clergy are silenced. The *opus Dei* is a bought product. The lady of the house has found a char to cook and clean for her husband. The lady of the house has sold out her own marriage rights and is left desolate. Now in the twentieth century must we wonder why men ask what the cathedral is for? "Why do these clergymen walk behind the vergers?" When we hear their services in our home on the radio and see them on the television it is the choir we follow, and they announce the name of the chief musician. Have they no parish clerk to read a lesson?

S. S. Wesley felt deeply for his Church. On May 24th 1849 he told a gathering of organists and choirmasters: "In the days of King Edward the Sixth there were 114 in the Chapel Royal. There were 24 Chaplains skilled in music. The race of voiceless and incompetent priests was not then known, everywhere the choirs were full of singers . . . Deans had not tasted the sweets of choir plunder." Lay clerks now went "cringing to the Dean's butler as an acknowledged superior" and "took orders from the Residentiaries' footman". Wesley also looked ahead. What of the men being trained in Oxford who go into Christ Church there and find "one man in a surplice"? It hurt to be reminded of the derisive laughter in the House of Lords during the passing of the Cathedral Measure, when one peer remarked, "We do not wish to tax the musical ability of the Minor Canons."[8]

Wesley went on to point out that you cannot sing church music without a big enough choir to sing antiphonally. The singing of Hebrew psalmody makes antiphony a *sine qua non*. One cannot sing church music without a chorus. Better to say perhaps that a chorus is essential to the liturgy and the office. What powerful unison song was once heard in our Gothic cathedrals with thirty or forty voices moving in a single psalmodic undulation. St. Paul's, Wesley reminds us, had once forty-two men and now sings with six. Anthems, he says, have ceased to be choral and are now written to show off soloists and are "more like glees". And for Wesley, when did this rot set in? After Elizabeth I when clergy began to "preach at choirs". Indeed the residentiaries were Dives and the musicians, it seems, Lazarus. Christian song, in their day to day life, must have been a hard thing for them. Wesley's father had published a beautiful service. Only one cathedral purchased copies. The plates were melted down. Attwood had had to buy his own choir music from his meagre salary.

There were others who had a discerning eye and ear without the fire and thrust of Samuel Sebastian Wesley.

Robert Whiston grievously noted that under the statutes of Henry VIII poor scholars were to receive £4; now they received but £1 8s. 4d. Prebendaries under the same statute were to receive £40; they now received £900.[9]

Dr. William Spark enjoyed his visit to St. George's Roman Catholic cathedral, mentioned earlier. He went to vespers on December 29th 1850. He paid 6d. at the door, though he could have got in for 3d. with a poorer view. He thought the music of Mozart most beautiful, but "inappropriate to the worship of God". He seems, with Boyce and Tudway, Gibbons and Tallis, to have had that sense of dignity which English church music naturally doth require.

On Sunday mornings Spark was accustomed to have his *Venite* sung and psalms read. He did not like the organ booming out a sung *Gloria* after a said psalm. (Psalms were sung at evensong.) He did not like the psalms mutilated by reading. "I must confess that when I go into any church where there is a tolerably good organ and choir and hear such verses in the psalms read as 'sing we merrily unto God our strength' . . . I feel they are not given in the spirit of the psalmist and are indeed robbed of half their power and effect."[10]

Spark was speaking of a parish church in Leeds in mid-Victorian times. At Shrewsbury in 1851 the clergy of the rural decanal chapter listen to W.H.H. encouraging them to form surpliced choirs—"Boys are better than quartets and surplices produce order"—and so end gallery indiscipline. The new custom of singing a hymn before the office he did not like. He points out that it is contrary to the rubric and destroys the intention of the Prayer Book order.[11]

Again W.H.H. complains of the new habit of singing a hymn after the sermon (an improper custom still very commonly with us). "A needless blow," he says, "to any impression the sermon might have made." The speed at which musical parts of the service were sung was generally too slow, destroying the nature of Christian song which

ought to be "joyful". Symphonies on the organ between
verses of hymns were "bad". Most important and least
heeded of all his comments was that on the new double
chant for psalms. The chants were going "higher and
higher". D he said was as high as you should go, and B for a
reciting note. If Shrewsbury listened, nobody else did. After
a century of this we inherit today a whole race of males
who have lost all voice or desire to sing in psalms. For too
long psalmody has been out of their reach (except for
musical enthusiasts). They have never known the opportunity for emotional involvement in the singing of a psalm in
church. Hebrew psalmody without emotion is like parsley
without sauce. Effeminacy which can cope with an Anglican
high double chant has taken over, not only the song, but
also the pew, in the mid twentieth century. What male
gladly tolerates so much overwhelming expression before
him by Eve?

W.H.H. was not alone in his *cri de coeur*. Another anonymous author of 1849 complains of harmonies. Melody in the
ladies' (treble) line only restricts the male. Tunes are pitched
too high. They use "airy" chants. The substitution in parish
churches of fancy service settings for chants restricts one
further. There is a "new" theory that choirs are "representative". From Day (1560), Tallis and Barnard to Clifford
and Boyce all responses have been the same. Now he
complains that one cannot always join in these for their
elaborate ideas. Responses, he appeals, *must* have the tune
in "the tenor". Psalms should begin with unison verses to
get the people going. Already the pointed psalter was
beginning what a later generation were to call the
"cathedral thump".[12]

THE OXFORD MOVEMENT AND THE OFFICE

The daily office was soon to become a parish church pecu-
liarity, a party badge, an eccentricity. The Rector of

Westborne, Sussex, in 1852 reports that the Bishop of —
interviewing Mr. — in connection with a vacant living
chanced to hear the unfortunate clerk use the phrase "the
daily service". The Bishop interjected, "I am sorry to tell
you that in that case it will be my *duty* not to present you . . .
I must discourage it."[13]

In places the Church went underground. Victorian piety
enabled some to continue to say the office in their homes.
Church buildings being shut and cold hearted, they presented themselves, prayer books in hand, as a family in the
drawing room, with the servants, after breakfast. One
Devon family met in the schoolroom at 8.0 and then "we
read round by turns, the psalms and lessons of the day".[14]

From these glimpses of the parochial organist, the
parochial parson, the parochial choir and the ever-
disappointed parochial laity, we may return now to the
cathedrals and see John Keble's "Assize Sermon" of July
14th 1833 begin to take effect. One of the first appointments
influenced by the Oxford Movement was that of Robert
Gregory to a canonry in St. Paul's in December 1868. He
admitted he had read *The Tracts for the Times*. He had heard
Newman preach his farewell sermon at Littlemore in 1843.
He was trained as an assistant curate by John's brother Tom
Keble, whom he claimed was the first parish priest to
revive the public recitation of the office both morning and
evening in a parish church.[15]

The day Gregory was installed in his canonry by Archdeacon Hale and the verger, the cathedral was dark, lit only
by a wax taper. The would-be congregation from his former
parish was locked outside. The new canon seems to have
decided instantly that, if he had anything to do with it,
things would change at St. Paul's. Nevertheless, it was
Henry Parry Liddon's appointment to a stall in 1870 that
led to an old chorister, John Stainer, being brought back
from Oxford in 1872. The latter days of the former organist,
Sir John Goss, were indeed unhappy days. "Only four adult

voices . . . anthem had to be changed . . . it cannot be allowed that any change should be made *during* the service." The organist was part-time, the choir was meagre and then invariably full of deputies. John Stainer took over a choir whose men had been quite unused to having rehearsals. He soon had both boys and men up to a realistic strength and, no doubt due to the influence of Gregory with Liddon, the boys were soon to be found wearing cassocks as well as surplices.

With the cassock came also the more formal entry and exit from liturgical worship. In 1843 the boys of the Abbey simply made their way in their own time to their places, awaiting the clock. In 1875 Dean Stanley is insisting that the choir exit slowly in front of him, proceeding via the west end of the church to the north door. One is left with a fairly clear impression of the dive and scramble for the cloisters which previously concluded the services. We must however recognise that this formality and dignity, although clearly very necessary at the time, was part of the contemporary pattern, with Victoria, Empress of India, etc., etc.[16]

In the twentieth century, other nations find very strange our military approach to prayer which we have inherited from the Victorians. Today the colours, races, tongues and religions which pour daily into that Abbey church to make up God's "one people" look upon this strange mystery. No other race approaches its God quite like this. Whilst we may admire the advantages and order of our custom, we must recognise that it undoubtedly hinders private devotion of those concerned both before and after service. This would not be so much a calamity if our order of service made some provision in its liturgical frame for private prayer. At Taizé it is now ordered that the brethren do not assemble in procession. The silence before service is one of four intentional liturgical silences. "In fact we love this space of silent preparation for prayer." We shall think about such matters again; here let us simply note that in fact we do little to help our regular clergy, choirmen and boys who are engaged in the routine of the daily office to acquire day by day personal at-one-ment. Little provision is made for a Dean to be caught up "in the spirit". We are terribly matter of fact, compared to our brethren of other parts of Christendom.[17]

Resulting from this "Great Britain" theology, or "Empire Day" form of devotion, there gets added at this period to the office, the vestry prayer, a new form of "count down". Piety and order are taking the place of carelessness and decay but opportunity in the Church of England to experience the "numinous" is rare, too rare in the daily office to be effective. The twentieth century, whilst enriching the ordered beauty, has so far added little to aid genuine religious experience.

Just as a family will clamber up to the dinner table on a routine day in an independent manner because it is a family, and not a barracks, so the ecclesiastical household in the twentieth century ought to consider whether our approach and departure from the daily office is in accord with our contemporary theological notions of "togetherness". Would it be more contemporary to give more place to the pente-costal fire and wind? The great international growth of sectarian pentecostalism must surely reflect ecclesiastical neglect, as all heresies and sects in all ages of the Church tend to do. Should the office continue to end with a decisive outflow of its executants rather like the final flush of a modern toilet? Has not prayer got more of the nature of a continuing and flowing stream?[18]

SOME CONCLUSIONS

It may be thought that far too much time has been taken up with the office in the cathedral. We cannot escape the fact that what is done in the cathedral today is done in all the greater parish churches tomorrow, and so in the lesser parish churches the day after. It is, of course, just as it should be. Martin Thornton insists that a cathedral office should be "unmutilated". He thinks "uniformity and continuity" are of first importance. He warns of the tendency to make the office in a cathedral a "snippet of organised religion" instead of an essential activity within the divine organism of a "world come of age".[19] Music must not come before objectivity or edification before praise.

It is therefore of much consequence to the whole Church in the United Kingdom that during the nineteenth century cathedral choirs improved to such an extent that they could sing high and "airy" chants to that significantly titled volume *The Cathedral Psalter*. How unfortunate that more and more tunes of hymns and psalms come to be the treble line to the exclusion of the male tenor. The Hymn Book in turn drove out the *Psalter* as the people's book of expressive divinity and much doubtful and wishy-washy theology expressed in its pages became the increasingly feminine diet of souls. It was an age of higher heels and higher voices in the parish church. It was indeed an age of more slender theology in worship.

The organ had displaced the band in the west gallery and reduced the opportunity of the amateur musician to make his sacrifice and offering with his fiddle. The barrel organ disappears and so does the chance of the machine over-stepping the psalm with an inadvertent "Little drops of brandy", followed by "Go to the devil and wash yourself", as during a service in Berwick in Sussex.[20] The diapason tone and volume on ever higher organ wind pressures gradually encourages the laity to be more and more lazy in their approach to the making of the office. Worship is generally to become feeble, though at St. Oswald's, Durham, where John Bacchus Dykes had his people really singing his "Jesu, Lover of my soul", or "Lead, kindly Light", a new look takes over in the parish office. These hymns and others like them really became evensong for the people. The canonical form was in fact generally rendered by the surpliced choir. John Stainer's *Cathedral Psalter* became as much a part of every village church as the Book of Common Prayer.

Meanwhile "Great Paul" was hung in 1882 in the southern tower at St. Paul's. Cannon Liddon's inscription was put upon it, *"Vae mihi si non evangelisavero"*—"Woe is unto me, if I preach not the gospel" (1 Cor. 9. 16). This was to be the clarion call to the Church at large.[21] The musicians were to have a good go at trying to do it. Throughout the century, within the cathedral lofts and in the village chancel there had been much true Christian gallantry, but deep repercussions were to be felt in the twentieth century when the Church discovered it had acquired an artificial superficiality, and the nation asked the Church, "Where is our spirituality?" Much that we find in church tends to be sub-Christian aesthetic beauty or, where less refined, a style of entertainment.

CHAPTER NINE

Parson, People and the Opus Dei in the Twentieth Century

An article was contributed to *Theology* in December 1963 under the title "The future of Mattins and Evensong" by Bishop Leslie S. Hunter. He returned from a visit to Taizé animated with a desire to see the clergy of the Church of England engaged again in live liturgy. Taizé also inspired Dom L. Lelois, O.S.B. to write, "I was inspired by finding how much greater emphasis was laid on quality than quantity in the structure of their Office"; and the monk goes on to quote Evagrius, "Do not take a delight in the multiplicity of psalms". Dom Lelois also quotes Symeon the New Theologian: "A single trisagion said with devotion and recollection before going to sleep is worth more than a four hour vigil of empty phrases."[1] Dr. Hunter's reactions to Taizé were not dissimilar. One of his conclusions was that the Psalter done "in course" is an unintelligent liturgical device.

Two sub-headings of Dr. Hunter's article were "Daily Offices for the Clergy" and "Mattins and Evensong on Sundays". Now does Dr. Hunter, with other liturgical reformers, begin to assume that we need a daily office for the clergy and a weekly office for the laity? This seems completely contrary to the sixteenth-century English reformers' ideal of the primitive Church and the Book of Common Prayer. Are parson and people to be engaged in one activity of public worship, or are new reforms to make the liturgical gap between cleric and laity wider than ever? There are two matters which need to be decided now. (a) Will the laity ever come again to join in the continuous divine office or is this a pious mirage? (b) Do the secular clergy in fact suffer from spiritual starvation, because of the form of the daily office?

THE LAITY AND THE CAVIAR

This is not a problem peculiar to the Anglican. H. A. Reinhold, an American Roman Catholic, writes under the heading of "Cloister and Society" of laity " . . . sitting patiently through the Sunday Masses saying their Rosaries —singing popular hymns . . . " He asks if the liturgy could not become the daily bread of the ordinary Catholic or was it to be caviar for the *élite*? Must there continue always to be a clerical track for expresses to heaven, while lay people rode slow freight trains with popular devotions that had little in common with the things behind the altar rail . . . [2]

Hans Kung, in his important book *The Living Church*, devotes a chapter to the "Importance of Liturgical Reform for Christian Unity". He goes on to ask for "A renewal service of the Word *of the entire Christian people*". He suggests a return to "particular emphasis on the morning and evening Hours". He asks for readings, exposition, "*singing of psalms*" and prayers. Then, turning his mind from the laity to the parish priest, he asks that his prayer may not "consist of saying a great number of words". The priest who carries out his work "under the pressure of modern conditions" must have "necessary time for God", be "quite free for God", apart from the regulation of a "definite number of words". He wants the priest "to pray the Psalms by heart in his own language". He declares: "A renewal of liturgical prayer would have a significant effect on the renewal of the Church as a whole, and there is no need for a lengthy explanation to show that it would also play an essential part in the movement of Christian reunion."[3]

Dom Wilfred Tuninek tells us that at the Monastery of

Mount Saviour in the U.S.A. they have been able to increase the amount of silence in the offices, without lengthening the service times, by rearranging the Psalter and omitting repetitions.[4]

Others have sought to revive the rich organic life for the laity; monks of the Abbey of Berne have produced a simple breviary. It contains a whole school of useful canticles and psalmody with instructive psalm headings and the Psalter reduced to a hundred and nine psalms, cut to length for uniformity, three short psalms being the dose. The calendar brings into relief Psalm 3 for martyrs, "I will not be afraid for ten thousands of the people", and Psalm 19, "Their sound is gone out into all lands", for apostles etc. Pope Paul, as Cardinal Montini, writing from the Vatican on November 15th 1962 says " . . . a long cherished hope has now been realised". Now this is nothing else but a book of Common Prayer for the Roman Communion, common in spirit and intention, that the laity should share the daily offices. A "long cherished hope" but still "a pious mirage"?[5]

Joseph Jungmann, S.J. well sees that although the laity may now be encouraged to join in the daily offices by the constitution on the liturgy, the proper provisions are not made: "The present state of affairs is simply the result of the fact that the Office, as it has been handed down in the West, has been a purely clerical liturgy for a long time." (Though he points out that in the East (Iraq) congregations still attend mattins and vespers daily.)

In his assessment of the primitive, unclericalised office, Jungmann suggests a simple shape in four phases: (a) "a reader announces God's message"; (b) "singing—re-echo the glad tidings"; (c) "the prayer of the people, said silently or spoken aloud in alternating choirs"; (d) "the priest— Christ's representative—alone utters the summarizing and concluding prayer which is therefore called the collect. In measured, well-tuned phrases he offers up to God the corporate prayer of the whole people".[6]

We have no great difficulty in discovering the daily common prayer of the (Church priest and laity) of Hilary or of Chrysostom, or Ambrose. "What can be more powerful and alluring than the confession of the Trinity, which is *daily sung* by the mouth of the people."[7] Jungmann has shown that the Church of St. Augustine of Hippo had a daily office but no certain daily mass.[8]

The Dean of Chester (as I pointed out in Chapter two) has asked for a modern adaptation of the large ancient parish churches, so that clergy, lay staff and people can work together and pray together to fight twentieth-century secularism. "That prayer would include the public recitation of the daily prayers of the Church *in a form in which the parish could join.*" In my own parish (a large English village), Evensong is normally *sung* in part every day. There may be a handful of confirmation candidates, the Mothers' Union, a few choirboys, simply the clergy or just the odd one or two laymen alone. Secularism cannot be fought with Sunday morning religion. The daily office of the village church must be at the heart of all reform. To cut into the Book of Common Prayer and make part "Sundays and people" and part "weekdays and parson" would be to destroy not only Cranmer's objective but the *opus Dei* itself.

I have briefly shown here that American, Belgian, German and Italian priests, as well as we in England, are all concerned about the present failure of the daily office to be the Church at its daily work. The association of the laity with the daily office should be no mirage in the evangelism of the industrial civilisation.

SOUL-STARVED PRIESTS

There is no doubt that, in pin-pointing the need to care for the soul of the priest, Dr. Hunter puts his finger on the truth. It is manifestly clear that many clergy neither ring the bell nor open the door. The Prayer Book has not held them.

Another school has begun the daily mass and created a list of "Intentions" to brighten up the uniformity! The 1928 Prayer Book, with its Specials for Virgins and "at the burial of the dead" can help to make it live. H. A. Reinhold writes of his Roman Catholic brethren: "What really happens is that the hardworking and the less strenuously occupied read the Office before they retire, sleepy and drained of all concentration, to get it over with. As their prayer life is centred around meditation, examination of conscience, visits to the Tabernacle, Rosary, Stations of the Cross, as solid bases of their spirituality, they are fed to satiety and the Office comes in as a cross to be borne in obedience . . . "[9]

Dietrich Bonhoeffer in *Life Together* cries out also for a live daily office. "Common life under the Word begins the common worship at the beginning of the day . . . the deep stillness of morning is first broken by the prayer and *song* of the fellowship. After the silence of night and early morning, hymns and word of God are more easily grasped." Bonhoeffer goes on to say that whether the congregation is a family or a college the pattern must be the same: scripture, *hymn*, prayer. The hymn of course *must* be *sung*. "The fact that we do not speak it but sing it only expresses the fact that our spoken words are inadequate to express what we want to say, that the burden of our song goes beyond all human words."[10]

We, with the Roman Catholic clergy, Lutherans and others, have a common problem. The beauty of the *opus Dei* has become dry bread. Our younger clergy look to the liturgical commissioners for release from so plain a diet. Was it not that the Psalter used to be the jam?

STERILE PERFORMANCES

The daily office book of Taizé may be compared with the suggested reforms of the breviary by H. A. Reinhold which take account of the "twentieth century rhythm of life".

7

He suggests:

mattins and lauds	twenty minutes' reading of morning prayer, and meditation
short prime	thanksgiving after mass and preparation for work
terce, sext and none	a recitation by heart of a psalm or hymn, chapter and Lord's Prayer
vespers and compline	fifteen minutes of prayer before bed

Reinhold continues: "These recommended devotions and the practice of walking in the presence of God—would by itself be a great help to consecrated lives without the burden of 'sterile performances' imposed and half resented . . . At least all clerics of goodwill would have a chance to be spiritual men—the grace of this office giving them strength to do less—better. *The greatest problem as I see it now, is the use of the Psalms.* It is an ill understood loyalty to the sacred Scriptures to evaluate them all alike."[11]

The Taizé community have already had to face this problem, and whilst aiming at a recitation of the whole psalter every six weeks have in fact bracketed the Marriage Psalm (Ps. 128), the imprecations (e.g. Ps. 79), and raised the question of the merits of saying the long historical psalms.[12] But Bishop Walter Frere, in publishing his *Liturgical Psalter* in 1925, went much further than Taizé has done. Unlike the latter he was concerned with secular common prayer, not a community at prayer. "The aim," he says, "has been not so much to remove what seemed unsuitable, as to choose what was most suitable, and to include whatever could most justly claim to be congregational and devotional."[13]

The Anglican Bishop Frere finds an ally in the Jesuit liturgist J. A. Jungmann, who asks for "a selection of those Psalms which the worshippers could say in adoration and supplication". "Few," he says, "can defend the old principle of the Psalms in course today." In discussing the origin of mattins he shows that lessons, canticles and prayers form the heart of the office, and that antiphonal psalmody comes in later as an extra to keep the people happy and occupied while they assembled.[14] Thus psalmody "in course" was not a primitive custom, as I have shown in Chapter Six. Though the Church in England may wish to be loyal to Cranmer, it ought not to stagnate under a loyalty to the mistaken, historical notions of his age.

Strangely enough Dietrich Bonhoeffer is one modern voice calling for psalmody "in course". In *Das Gebetbuch der Bible: Eine Entführung in Die Psalmen* (1940) he pleads for a recovery of the Psalter in his own Church. We should not, he says, pick and choose, but pray *all* the psalms.[15] He is able in prison to reap great personal strength from the silent ordered recitation. Nobody will deny that such a man, accustomed to teaching, has the mental ability to do the Christological acrobatics. Their use "in course" for private meditation is one thing. Their use "in course" in the Book of Common Prayer for liturgical song by manual workers is quite another.

Jungmann points out that the Church "no longer requires the protection of rigidity". He shows that all the good things which were building up in Cardinal Quignon's Breviary in 1534 were stamped on by such as the Spiritual Canonist John of Arze in 1557, as dangerous innovations when the ship was already rocking.[16] By the same token the Elizabethan Acts of Uniformity are no longer required by the Anglican as a rock of defence against a Protestant underworld. *Rigidity must, in the new ecumenical atmosphere, give place to prayer.*

UNSHACKLE THE PSALTER

The monthly cycle "in course" must be changed for the Anglican priest, and the weekly cycle for the Roman Catholic. The old traditional Trinity for Monday, Angels for Tuesday, Mary for Saturday will not do; nor will the Faith, Hope, Love, etc. of the 1680 breviary. The 1928

Order for Sunday Use has caused the Anglican system to fall like a pack of cards. Since the known monthly cycle was tampered with, the layman has been utterly at sea, not knowing why he sings what or when. We were warned by Bishop Walter Frere that this would happen. As early as 1925 he wrote that the proposed attempt to put nearly all the psalms into the Sunday pattern, one after another, was "a hankering after the discarded ideal".[17] We all appear now to be in need of an ordered freedom in psalmody, where the abbot, the dean, the vicar or the missionary (in the bush or on the housing estate) can dip in for what he or his people need. Much of what he takes out must be sung, and much of this is unison song, to which Dietrich Bonhoeffer recalls us.[18] Reading will not do. What can be more stupid than to hear a clergy chapter begin their office —"O Lord, open thou our lips", "O come, let us sing"—and then go on to grunt and mutter?

Dom Aldhelm Dean writes: "If on New Year's Night the dancers solemnly stand round the room, hands crossed, and recite 'Should auld acquaintance be forgot' can it be said to have the same depth of meaning"? So "with the Choir Office, we cannot be said to be giving of our best to God if we merely recite what with a shade more generosity, we could easily sing."[19]

It would appear that an annual cycle of psalmody can be the only form that can be made to fit the requirements of the twentieth-century working man. In some ways, the principles and purpose behind the proposals I make in Chapter Ten are similar to those made by Harold Riley in *The Revision of the Psalter* (1948). Today, however, we are beginning to think much more about the vocation of the laity than was then the case. The suggestions which follow will be found to be more of the nature of "Common Prayer" than the nature of a revised breviary (cf. Chapter Thirteen). The psalms as hereafter detailed will form a pattern of introits and graduals to the daily reading and Prayer of

Priests and People. As regards Sundays, the old joys of Psalm 93, *"Dominus Regnavit"* ("The Lord is King"), etc. will have to suffer extinction except in collegiate or monastic foundations, where all are together daily. The Sunday Psalter will be governed for most of us by the season, as is the collect, epistle and gospel. The Psalter will become again a hymn book to go with the "Intention". (One may compare here Bishop Frere's suggestions in his work *Some Principles of Liturgical Reform*.)[20] There will be the Jeremiahs who will think that in this way all we shall get is the Vicar's favourite half-dozen psalms. No; unshackle the Psalter and "the Singing Church" will sing again.

Such an idea of tampering with the order of psalmody is no rash new thing. The need to bring more life and meaning has been long felt, but reform has invariably been postponed.

When Convocation re-emerged in 1852 into an active body Prayer Book reform was one of the first of its problems (1854). The Committee's report called for "On ordinary weekdays a shorter order for daily prayer (3)". The report was rejected.

In 1861 the Dean of Norwich moved in the Lower House that a Commission be set up to look into "(3) a rearrangement of the Psalter".

J. M. Neale, writing in *The Ecclesiologist* in 1856, asked for "Proper psalms for a greater number of festivals and feasts" and said "the Church was forgetting the use of the Psalter as a manual of devotion".[21]

The proposals of Convocation in 1879 were to allow an increase in proper psalmody, but had they come into effect they would have done no more than the reforms of 1928, i.e. rupture one system without creating another. Bishop Walter Frere had asked in 1925 for a "selective plan" of psalmody, a "liturgical psalter", and pointed out that "nowhere else in Christendom do ordinary lay people attempt . . . this continuous recitation". Unfortunately the Church of England rejected then this study in psalms of a great liturgical and musical scholar.

CHAPTER TEN

A Psalter Arranged for Song

REVISIONS COMPARED

Many will be alarmed at the thought of an annual cycle of psalmody and will immediately dismiss the proposition as being too sparse to merit consideration. Let me allay some fears.

In the plan given in the Appendix is provided a daily morning psalm, a communion psalm, an evening psalm. Thus the ration will be three in a day rather than the present Church of England average of five in a day, plus *Venite*. This is intentional: that we should do less, better. As in Quignon's Breviary, and as already expressed by Bonhoeffer, it is intended to put the heavier rations on the morning when the mind is less pressed.

I have kept to the uneven quantities of whole psalms rather than to several equal portions of a dissected psalmody, as in *The Little Breviary* of the monks of Berne, because (a) I believe this to be a more truly Anglican and biblical way of worship and (b) as poetry or lyrics most of the psalms stand or fall as separate artistic works.

The Liturgical Commission have produced a morning office which is after the manner of a pro-anaphora. Thus, whether there is a daily eucharist or not, a morning office on ferial days may soon displace the present Prayer Book order of mattins and Holy Communion and remove the undue weight on the parochial clergy, who at present often read *four* lessons before breakfast.

It will be seen that the morning introit psalms are chosen on a monthly basis, as was the reformed Anglican pattern (1662). They become a daily song and meditation on awakening, drawn from traditional sources; thus, on the Tenth Day of the month Psalm 50 would be sung, "The Lord . . . called the world, from the rising up of the sun", following the Gregorian medieval use.

Meanwhile the second psalm in the morning in the anaphora is chosen on a weekly basis to go with the theme for the Sunday. Thus the gospel for the First Sunday after Epiphany has "Now his parents went to Jerusalem" and the psalm for the week is 122, "Our feet shall stand in thy gates: O Jerusalem".

Generally speaking, these communion psalms will be recited only seven times in the year instead of twelve, as is the current practice. Nevertheless I believe they will be better known and loved than they are at present because the meanings will often be the more imprinted on the memory by the other associations with the Church Calendar. One is also to hope that after the psalm has been sung in church on Sunday to a tune, the tune may help to carry it on in the home during the week that follows, in much the same way as older people continue the use by memory of the Sunday collect. In Church primary schools something might be done with this, when the psalms are not long. The clergy meanwhile may also be aided to sing on Monday and Tuesday what the choir sang on Sunday.

In the medieval use the particular meaning of the psalm was brought out by the antiphon. You knew where you were going: "The prism of the Church separated the colourless light into its component rays: into the violet of penitence, the crimson of martyrdom, the gold of the highest seasons of Christian gladness."[1] It does not seem that return to antiphons would be generally acceptable, despite the generous applause given to the Gelineau psalmody. Would it be too much to suggest a black line in the margin or a heavy type for verses where liturgical uses have been decided upon by Convocation?

There are several features in the scheme provided here which are similar to the one worked out in the *The Book of Common Worship* of the Church in South India.[2] C.S.I. provides a psalm to take its place appropriately between the Old Testament lection and the epistle of the day. Thus for the Third Sunday in Lent (forgiving one another) we have:

> Genesis 50. 15-21   Joseph and his brothers
> Psalm 15   "Lord, who shall dwell in thy tabernacle . . . ?"
> Colossians 3. 12-17   love, the bond of perfectness
> Matthew 18. 21-35   the two debtors

A person of reasonable intelligence will immediately see a point of relevance in singing this psalm. This is precisely what does not happen when on the Third Sunday in Lent in the current Church of England use the vicar gives out at mattins Psalm 119, verses 73–104. The same is ordered in Ceylon,[3] whilst the United States are no better off with Psalms 25 and 34.[4] The primary concern must be to show that the psalm is relevant and important.

Whilst the C.S.I. book and this one both agree in trying to provide a proper psalm again for the Sundays of the year, they differ in selection because (a) C.S.I. has a series of Old Testament lections to work on, and (b) C.S.I. still retains a daily recitation roughly according to numerical order (i.e. psalms in course for the daily offices). This book proposes the total abolition of psalms "in course", as being wrong in principle for public common prayer. C.S.I. juggles with the order to get evening psalms in the evening, etc. Thus Psalms 4 and 31 are kept to the evening of the First and Ninth Days instead of being on the First and Sixth Mornings as in the Church of England, whilst Psalm 5 is moved to the First Morning. The Cursing Psalms (e.g. 58) may be omitted by C.S.I. and two Messianic Psalms 2 and 110 grouped to-

gether on the Sixteenth Evening. The Book of Common
Prayer (U.S.A.) also attempts to be rational with natural
interpretations whilst retaining a complicated system of
"in course" recitation.

I have attempted to pull apart the Psalter into roughly
three liturgical uses: (a) the Calendar use (Holy Communion); (b) for the daily toil (mattins and evensong); (c)
for feasts and special times (occasional offices).

With this annual cycle a priest or layman will use ninety
psalms in the course of a month instead of his former
hundred and fifty. To these will be added those used in the
occasional offices. This does not seem an unreasonable
reduction for the twentieth-century priest, bearing in mind
the time available to his predecessor in the sixteenth century.

Let us summarise therefore what follows in this chapter,
and in the table in the Appendix.

Eleven psalms have been omitted, being unsuitable for
liturgical use, as in Bishop Frere's *Liturgical Psalter*. I would
refer those who doubt the wisdom of this to Dr. Frere's
book.[5]

Three psalms have been omitted as doubles. Surely only
the fool wants to say twice over "The fool hath said in his
heart" because it happens to be printed twice over.

Twenty-one psalms have been withdrawn from the
liturgical pattern. Some have been taken out because
psalmody in public worship is intended to be song, and they
are more suitable for recitation or private reading; some
because of their length, being an impossible strain on
the average church, though admirable in a cathedral,
where they may be added. Some have been withdrawn
because their thought is too incongruous to the modern congregation; some because they are essentially personal;
some because they are close repetitions of others. Those
clergy who would want to continue to recite a complete
Psalter should table those omitted and use them in daily
private meditation.

Thus fifty-three psalms find themselves as proper psalms for Sundays, etc., and will be repeated daily in the days that follow. Thirty are set apart for mattins and thirty for evensong. Eighteen are for Saints and occasional offices, there being a few repetitions. Of the psychological necessity of titles and the importance of production and print I have written elsewhere.

THE DAILY OFFICE PSALTER

Psalms for the daily offices have been chosen first on basic original meanings rather than mystical meanings. This is one of the necessary repercussions on liturgy of biblical criticism. In effect, the original proper psalms for morning and evening, of the Eastern Church and of the Western Church, have been wedded to form the basis of the scheme. The monthly cycle peculiar to Anglicans has been continued not only to make the changes more amenable to the clergy who have lived throughout their ministry with the monthly Psalter, but also because this forms the rough natural limit for psalms which were in origin morning and evening songs. It has been necessary to draw on the suggestions of Cardinal Quignon's Breviary, the very excellent Parisian use, and *The Little Breviary*, together with psalms in the Gregorian use which were really part of psalms "in course", to round up the figure. The month ends with the Eastern daily *Ainoi* (148–150) at mattins, which is also part of the daily Western use. In this way the Anglican returns in fact nearer to primitive use and even Jewish custom, as Cranmer would have wished.

The priest at monthly prayer with these psalms will be joining in common morning and evening prayer not only with his Roman brethren in vespers and compline, but on certain days he will be in union with the Eastern monk in his *Orthros* and *Mesorian* of prime. He will also be keeping, for the most part, to the wisdom of the Fathers in the

Council of Laodicea who decreed that only one psalm be sung at one time.

THE EUCHARISTIC PSALTER

The eucharistic psalm will be much used by the laity if the parish communion form of worship continues to gain ground. It therefore attempts to be a cross section of the whole Psalter, giving a considerable weight of Old Testament teaching which is so lacking in much popular modern devotion. It contains the original eucharistic psalms used in the Early Church by Origen, Cyril and Augustine (e.g. 26 and 34). It contains the psalms used in the Orthodox liturgy at the present time (103 and 146), that of the 1570 Roman Missal (43), and the modern Roman use of Psalms 84, 85 and 116. It may therefore be said to be truly ecumenical in spirit.

For the great festivals the most telling of the proper psalms have been selected, it being borne in mind that most people will come to church only once at Christmas and, hearing the one same psalm year by year (if sung to the same tune), they will come to appreciate their psalmody as seasonal as they do already the hymns. In some cases the proper psalms have been spread over into the seasonal weeks; for example Psalm 114 (a proper for Easter in 1662) goes to the Sunday after Easter, and Psalm 145 (a proper for Whit-Sunday in 1662) goes to Trinity II. (I am sure one reason why our pentecostal joy and our missionary zeal is so pent up in the Church of England is because the Prayer Book, on account of its historical origins, has so little to offer us in this field. The fire and wind blow out as quickly as they come, with Trinity Sunday tending to be a fire extinguisher.) The tradition of singing Psalm 119 in Trinity has been followed.

The 1549 introit psalms seem to have been an attempt to marry psalms to the gospels. It appears to me to have been made in a hurry, though Dean Addleshaw says "as a rule the psalm fits admirably". Bishop Frere concluded that "a special psalm was chosen for certain days, when there seemed to be a reason for choice; but on other days the psalmody followed something like a course". Whilst following the 1549 principle in general, a new scheme has been worked out suggesting at least a simple point of common mind between psalm and epistle or gospel, psalms that are not suitable for daily mattins or evensong generally being selected.[6]

The Church in Wales has recently put forward a similar table of eucharistic psalms, well thought out in the context of the lesson or epistle. Thus in Wales they may, on the feast of the Presentation of Christ, sing out:

"We wait for thy loving-kindness, O God:
in the midst of thy temple"

and on St. David's Day, Wales thinks it well that one David should say to the other:

"The lot is fallen unto me in a fair ground:
yea, I have a goodly heritage."[7]

It will be found that as a general rule these eucharistic psalms will be best sung as a gradual, for two reasons.

First, this is the original place of psalmody in the mass, whereas introits and communion psalms, etc., were a later addition.

Second, the discursive nature of many of the psalms will come well as a meditation, immediately prior to the gospel, whereas the introit needs to be more chorus in its purpose of binding the congregation together.

As I have said earlier, whole psalms have been taken in preference to snippets. The clergy will more easily accept this change if it includes whole psalms. Obviously many small parishes will be unable to cope with some of the longer ones, though on the whole they are short. Parishes will need to tailor the scheme to fit their abilities. A town church with choir has been the norm in mind.

Before leaving the eucharistic uses I quote a further example. For Trinity XI the gospel is the story of the pharisee and the publican. The psalm suggested to match this is the Pilgrim Psalm (84) which includes "My soul hath a desire and longing to enter into the courts of the Lord".

THE PSALTER FOR SAINTS AND OCCASIONAL OFFICES

Psalms as "propers for Saints" are much needed now that the 1928 form of Prayer Book with its propers for black lettered Saints becomes more and more generally adopted in the various provinces of the Anglican Communion. What is provided here is nothing more than a skeleton, but at the same time if these are to be sung by small numbers on week-days which are Saint's Days, they will need to be well known, and are therefore best often repeated.

Thus the suggestion of the monks of Berne for feast days of Apostles is followed from their *Little Breviary*—Psalm 19, for example, which includes "Their sound is gone out into all lands". For Martyrs, St. Clement of Alexandria has suggested Psalm 124, which includes "Our soul is escaped even as a bird".

The psalms for funerals have been enlarged to take in pre-Reformation usage. Thus the 23rd Psalm comes back in from the Armenian and Gregorian usage; Psalm 130 and 139 also, as suggested in *The Alternative Services*; *Series II* (1965).

I cannot, however, subscribe to the use of Psalm 121 at funerals as proposed in the *Series II*. Indeed there is ample biblical suggestion that life after death is a journey, for example John 14. 2, "In my Father's house are many resting places" (μοναι). Thus the Traveller's Psalm might be suitable were the office not to conclude with the words of Blessed John that "Blessed are the dead which die in the Lord . . . that they may rest from their labours" (Rev.

14. 13). This condition of the joy of rest is often so fitting and apt. It doesn't mix well with Psalm 121 with its "going out" and "coming in", being more of the type of journey undertaken by the business executive.

Psalms 23, 90, 130, 139 cover (as the 1662 use did not) all ages in death. Brevity is provided for in necessity. It is important that rich or poor, famous or infamous, saints and sinners, be in death treated alike by Holy Church. An office of composed dignity is provided. It is better that such glory or shame as may be natural should be read into the liturgy as it stands by those enjoined in offering the same, rather than clerical, spur of the moment, compositions should prejudge the Almighty's disposition regarding the corpse present.

The unwonted liberties taken with the Prayer Book psalms at royal weddings by archbishops has led to a wholesale sentimentality over wedding psalms (Psalm 23 with its reference to the shadow of death being a most popular choice). It has been felt that the two proper psalms 128 and 67, so ordered (1662) for young women, and women past child bearing, are both adequate and beautiful to the occasion, and nothing is to be gained by multiplying these.

It is assumed that since the basis of the scheme is the parochial unit, the clergy and more faithful laity will all use the occasional offices from time to time. Psalms quoted as propers for Saints and occasional offices have not therefore all been repeated in the annual cycle.

THE MEMORY AND THE SPIRITUAL LIFE

Robert Bridges wrote, "No one can sing the psalms who does not know them by heart. All he can be expected to do is to follow."[8] Only after they are in the memory are they useful for communion with God. The Anglican clergy say their psalms once a month; twelve times a year; a hundred and twenty times in ten years; and yet comparatively few of us can recite a psalter well from memory even after a lifetime. This shows that something is wrong. Most of us, a few years after ordination, feel that we become wedded to the monthly course and enjoy it. Let us, all the same, face the fact that we do not know in our minds and prayers the psalms, despite constant repetition. Now if they are to be remembered by the people they must have individuality of thought, of music, and probably of purpose.

The spiritual value of knowing the psalms, or some psalms, by heart cannot be overstressed. Only constant repetition under like situations will achieve this, and only when it is achieved do the psalms begin to be of use in the vocabulary of religious experience.

To aid the memory it is necessary to break down the Psalter into its varieties of poetic shape and pattern, to stress paragraphs, choruses and refrains. In 1879 Bishop Westcott at Durham produced a psalter along such lines. Editors since have taken little notice of the advances he developed.[9]

"It is evident," Westcott wrote in the introduction, "upon the least reflection that no one uniform method of chanting can be applicable to the whole psalter. Sometimes the verses are separately complete; sometimes they are arranged in couplets, sometimes in triplets; sometimes they are grouped in unequal but corresponding masses. In most cases the verses consist of two members but not infrequently they consist of three or four. If therefore the psalms are sung antiphonally on one method of single verses or in pairs of verses or in half verses, the sense must constantly be sacrificed; and the music instead of illuminating the thought will fatally obscure it."

Antiphonal singing (i.e. singing by alternate choirs or voices) in some form or grouping is essential to a great many psalms, and some pointing device must be found to separate, for example, the call in Psalm 24, "Who is the King of glory" or the repeating refrain in Psalm 107, "So when they cried . . . " It is nonsense to expect people to use the psalms for ten years before they discover the shape, when modern ability to read and look at a printed page can tell one at a glance the shape of the poetic pattern.

When a psalter is printed for singing in choir, as in a Book of Common Prayer, it should only have commas where a break in singing or recitation is required, or better still no commas at all, as in the Worcester book.[10] In the new *Revised Psalter* for the Church of England, pointed for congregations, we have made a start towards providing a book for congregational singing,[11] but its print and format are miserably poor. It looks too much like the foreign affairs page of *The Times*. The Church continues to forget that a far greater number of its potential congregation are more at home with the front page of the *Daily Mirror*.

In the better days of the "Singing Church" antiphony was the normal way of "doing David" in the parish church. A single example from the duties of the second deacon as laid down in the constitutions of Trinity Church, Coventry, in 1462 will suffice: "He shall sing in the choir daily services on the same north side if it be a Sunday or Holy Day he shall be rector and begin all the psalms for that side of the choir."[12] We, in churches today, must not be too scared of antiphony which forces upon people their responsibility to sing. They will thank us for it in time.

To stir the memory, a title is imperative. The biblical titles have amused scholars but are hopeless for the missionary. The title must be brief and captivating. It is not intended to be the sub-heading of a sermon, for example "An appeal for mercy and justice from one who is surrounded by malicious and crafty enemies" (*Worcester* Ps. 56), but simply a tag, like "A morning hymn" (*Worcester* Ps. 3).

Tunes are the vehicle of the memory. If you do not believe this try reciting "O come, all ye faithful" and see how far you get before the rhythm or sound of the tune *Adeste fideles* begins to take over. So it is the more important that tune and words be wedded to aid memory. Some

attempt has been made on a magnificent scale to do this in
The Anglican Chant Book: "wherever possible long established
associations have been retained".[13] The research of these
editors has been well worth while, but I cannot agree when
they say that their selection is "Suitable for general use in
parish churches". The standard of chants and their range is
far more at home in the cathedral than in the humdrum
town or village church.

Of course we may go on producing an effeminate church
if we wish. We persist in refusing to notice that hardly a man
in our congregations ever really lets himself go in a psalm.
Since it is not in the nature of a male to be a silent partner,
we do an injustice to his psychology if we expect him to
keep on returning to listen to the kids and ladies. The more
spiritual may return to pray, the more intellectual to listen,
the more obedient to do his duty, but this does not absolve
the clergy from their sin of neglect.

It is difficult to say when this effeminate rot began. It is
interesting, however, to read what Roger Bacon had to say
to the Pope about us in 1267. "But now in the Church there
grows up little by little an abusive chant which sounds not
low and manly and without shame lapses into softness and is
tamed and sends out a prohibited natural (alto), which is a
curious new harmony the slippery invention which produces
an absurd pleasure in the multitude of warblings. And above
all voices in falsetto falsify the strong and sacred harmony producing a purer noise and effeminate lax men allow the same
almost throughout all the church. I am able to expose the
example of all the great cathedral churches and other famous
colleges in which all the offices are confounded by this corruption which I have spoken of."[14] Was this the beginning?

Today, the pitch, breathing and musical intervals should
be such as require a minimum of effort, much as in a folk
tune. Many psalms are of the style of meditation, but most
choirmen, if pressed to sincerity, will reluctantly agree that
ninety per cent of their intention is devoted to the musical

8

conundrums. This proves that musically something is radically wrong.

In the matter of the method of psalmody I have advocated a return to early church custom. In the matter of tunes I shall advocate a return to early Anglican reformed custom.

John Merbecke in his *Book of Common Prayer Noted* in 1550 offered us a simple unison plainsong form based upon his understanding of English word forms, but hindered by the fact that the tunes known were suited to Latin endings.[15]

PSALM 6   1550

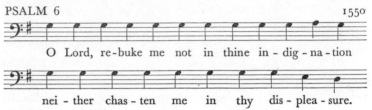

O Lord, re-buke me not in thine in - dig - na - tion

nei - ther chas - ten me in thy dis - plea - sure.

Then another generation came along, and, putting the plainsong tune in the tenor, hedged it in with alternative harmony.

CHRIST CHURCH TUNE, circa 1620

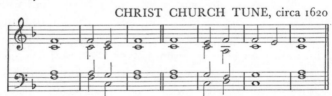

To make it all more interesting it became twice as long:

REV. LUKE FLINTOFT, circa 1720

but note the flowing and simple pattern of both tenor and
soprano. There is no ugliness, nor great musical skill needed
here. And so we come to look at this:

JOHN DAVY, circa 1800

and begin to see why psalmody in the Church of England
has become the prerogative of the choir. The tune, now in
the soprano, jumps about like a cat on hot bricks, and men
of the congregation were expected to sing a recitative on
top E! They couldn't, so they gave up singing psalms,
though they still mouth words as a token of good manners.
Even the old plainsong Tone VIII so often sung to Psalm 150
is invariably pitched as C. V. Stanford put it for cathedral
choirs, in C Major:

Circa 1900

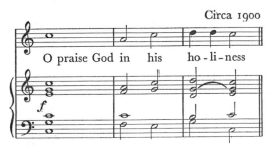

O praise God in   his   ho - li - ness

a good third higher than Cranmer and the monks sang it.

Tunes must, then, be set at a reasonable pitch for mascu-
line singing, say between E and A, and seldom depart too

far up or down, moving as a rule by pattern rather than interval. They must be able to stand on their own merit as themes without harmony or else they cannot be taken out of church and into the kitchen. We need in time to marry up chants to psalms so that each carries the character of the psalm. Then the work of memory can carry on, enabling the soul to grow in the experience of psalmody: as C. S. Lewis says, "fully God-centred—joyous to the highest degree, and unmistakably real".[16]

INTERPRETATION IN THE WIND OF CHANGE

From day to day somebody challenges the common sense of continuing to devote time in Christian worship to hearing the lurid stories of Hebrew warfare and the disgusting acts of murder or bigamy committed by most of the leading characters. This criticism is relevant to the Book of Psalms, though perhaps less strongly, since the breaking of children's skulls on stones is a comparatively rare feature (Ps. 137).

Professor C. D. F. Moule writing in *Theology*, October 1958, asked for a "radical purge" in the selection of psalmody for public worship. His estimate was that only seventy were "tolerable in Christian worship". Whilst agreeing in principle, I have followed Bishop Frere in abstracting from public worship a much smaller number.

It is very necessary to see worship on an international canvas. What may seem irrelevant in Washington can be close to the bone in Calcutta. "Shinto in Japan, the lower forms of Hinduism in India, the widespread practices of animism in S.E. Asia and on the African Continent give the battle between Jahwism and the Canaanite baal-worship a new significance." Bishop Kenneth Sansbury of the British Council of Churches goes on, "at a time when serious thinkers try to find an escape from materialism in the monism of Hindu thought or the high-minded agnosticism of Therewada Buddhism or alternatively commit themselves to secular humanism, the deepest affirmations of God's transcendence in the Old Testament . . . need to be grasped afresh . . . The New Testament does not affirm them with the same emphasis as the Old, just because it takes them for granted."[17]

Thus it is necessary at the frontier of mission to continue to experience the basic qualities of Hebrew spirituality. The frontier of mission is as close in the dehumanising areas of modern industrial cities as anywhere in the world.

At the turn of this century in a volume on the psalms entitled *The War-Songs of the Prince of Peace* R. M. Benson wrote, "Whether we say the Psalms publicly or privately, we must lose ourselves in Christ . . . As Circumcision is transformed into Baptism, and Jewish Sacrifices to Eucharistic Communion, so the Psalms of Davidic hope are transformed into the glowing utterances of Messianic perfection."[18]

I do not believe that this school of interpretation, then generally accepted, will now stand the test of our scientific age. It developed, as the early Church also developed, minutiae of allegorical interpretations and second meanings. It has been said, "Fanciful allegorism can suggest to modern man at best something unreal, at worst it can look like semantic cheating."[19] This does not mean that we can no longer accept the psalms as the songs of the Prince of Peace. It means that we must, for the most part, take them on their face value and offer them to God as the songs of humanity, a world mixed up in all David's sin and shame. "I feel sure," says C. S. Lewis, "that we must not either try to explain them away or to yield for one moment to the idea that, because it comes in the Bible, all this vindictive hatred must somehow be good and pious. The hatred is there— festering, gloating, undisguised . . . "[20] Between us and R. M. Benson is Belsen.

So when we sing Psalm 23 on the Seventh Morning of the month we mean no more and no less than that our God cares for us today and leads us forth in the right way; that as

humans we too may have such very unchristian attitudes as
to enjoy going out to dinner with a fine hair-do and an
excellent bottle, while those horrid Joneses have to look on.
Then when we say that we will "dwell in the house of the
Lord" we mean go to the church on the corner. All very dull
and horridly everyday—but this is just why the working man
in every generation finds the Psalter fits.

Again if we sing Psalm 128 at the wedding of the girl next
door, it is because we hope her husband will be a hard
worker and have success at his job. We would like the girl to
have babies which will grow up around the family table.
May your town not be forced on to the dole and we would
like you both to grow old together and have grandchildren.
(Benson wanted us to see in this psalm "The City of
Righteousness in her perpetuity".)

Some of the psalmody we shall interpret in this personal
and private manner, but to a much greater extent than
heretofore we will now see in the Psalter the community at
prayer, the cult of the Church. Traditional Jewish and
Christian interpretation has always regarded the psalms as
individual poetry. David has been considered as the semi-
divine originator. Scholars have spent lifetimes trying to
decide when or where in David's life this or that happened.
Sigmund Mowinckel has suggested that Roman Catholic
exegetes might well have arrived at a more cultic insight
into psalmody had they not been hindered by the dogmatic
presupposition of Davidic authorship. Biblical criticism has
now demonstrated that the psalms were not the work of one
or two men of one period. They have been shown to be the
product of a panorama of religious history. Further, they
are not for the most part personal compositions, but the
product of liturgical worship (the cult).[21]

Mowinckel cites Psalms 24, 68, 118 and 132 as obvious
examples of festival liturgical occasions, but he goes on to
prove that many that look like private prayers were in fact
used in the Temple liturgy. He cites for example Psalm 22,

"My God, my God . . . "; the soul is then poured out in verse 22, "in the midst of the congregation will I praise thee".

A long list of psalms have this reference in the midst of the text to the "congregation" or assembly. He or she had gathered with friends in the House of God. The choirman offered the song, the sacrifice might be offered—the community were a necessary part of the liturgical act, whether it was one of thanksgiving after illness or of royal deliverance in battle. (St. Paul's vow of Acts 21. 24 appears to be part of such a ritual.)

It is not my purpose here to examine this change of under-standing of psalm origins, but only to draw out its conse-quences. If we concede, with modern exegetes, that the great body of these psalms were of cultic origin, then it is the more necessary to use them within cultic worship and not regard them as a compendium of private devotions, the only corporate part of which is the discipline of co-ordinated recitation.

A brief word may be added about the part of the musicians in the cultic life of Hebrew religion. So many of the psalms allude to singing or instrumentation that, as Mowinckel says, "There can be no doubt that the psalms were meant to be sung".[22] The singers do not always seem to have been on the best of terms with the other staff of the House. They were not property owners but "sojourners in the gates of Israel",[23] sometimes descendants of slaves. They constantly speak of the poor and remarkably seldom mention the office of a priest. But psalm after psalm speaks of "the Temple" or its environs or furniture. The life work of the psalmist was to receive the people in God's holy place in trouble or in joy, to express their emotions for them, to offer them the comfort of "his wings" (Ps. 36. 9), "the well of life" (Ps. 36. 9) and send them forth in joy and peace of mind.

This same purpose must become our contemporary usage, the difference only being that we can sing for ourselves with the aid of a book. The Prayer Book revisers and liturgists must firmly grasp this total change of understanding concerning the style and origins of the psalms and apply their academic studies in this field to the needs of twentieth century devotional life.

The pattern of personal numerical recitation must pass away along with the concept of Davidic personal authorship. There are however those few psalms which the New Testament writers took up (understanding Davidic authorship) and in common used to testify unto Jesus the Christ. In particular, Psalms 2, 8, 22, 41, 69, 110 and 118 can never now be separated from the use the Evangelists made of them.[24]

CHAPTER ELEVEN

Worship in the Age of Din

THE QUESTION OF SILENCE

The measure Fahrenheit is in eclipse, because zero is the basis of the mathematician's reckoning. From here he comes and goes. The musician has to accept the unhappy fact that he begins and ends in silence—that when all is said and done the climax of his work is always the silence immediately post-dating his chord.

When the post-medieval romantics set the mass to sound, the moment of the holy, the moment of transubstantiation, is the moment of nihil. To "keep silence before him" is to be in tune with the Lord. So is God after all not the perfect "ding" but the perfect "shush"? (c.f. page 36) Otto puts Bach's *B Minor Mass* to the test. "Its most mystical portion is the 'Incarnatus' in the 'Credo', and there the effect is due to the faint, whispering, lingering sequence in the fugue structure, dying away pianissimo. The held breath and hushed sound of the passage, its weird cadences, sinking away in lessened thirds, its pauses and syncopations, and its rise and fall in astonishing semitones, which render so well the sense of awe-struck wonder—all this serves to express the mysterium by way of intimation, rather than a forthright utterance."[1]

"The Lord is in his holy temple: let all the earth keep silence before him" (Hab. 2. 20). The response of creation to the God who "moved" in the silence of the void and darkness (Gen. 1. 2) was that "the morning stars sang together, and all the sons of God shouted for joy" (Job 38.7). It was this response of creation that brought Job in chapter 42, verse 6 to "repent in dust and ashes". The response of creation to the movement from silence, must also be the response of man to the movement from silence. The christian's daily office must have some point of zero, of nihil, from which the created being responds to the creator. The sense of God cannot be taught. Man cannot be educated to experience the numinous, "it can only be evoked, awakened in the mind; as everything that comes 'of the spirit' must be awakened".[2]

The power of music to carry man forth from the point of nihil to the point of shouting for joy is no new thing, but the Church takes little heed. "From music goes forth," says Goethe, "an all mastering efficacy, of which, however, no man is able to give an account. Religious worship cannot therefore do without music. It is one of the foremost means to work upon men with an effect of marvel."[3]

The architect plays on light in the clerestory of the Gothic cathedral to show God is light. The basic form of creation is the darkness. "In him was life; and the life was the light of men. And the light shineth in darkness" (John 1. 4, 5). The architectural basic form is darkness, the created blob of matter. The light is of the life of God. God said, "Let there be light." Did God not also say, "Let there be sound"?

The finding of God in sound will not be according to the volume of sound, the rhythm or the pitch, but according to the awe or dread. "It may steal upon him almost unobserved as the gentlest of agitations, a mere fleeting shadow passing across his mood. It has therefore nothing to do with intensity . . . "[4]

Professor Otto discusses the numinous. He accepts with Luther that "the natural man" who has no fear has no God. For God is only understood when the natural man accepts that there is "the other", that the other exists; and as the

sex instinct comes up at him as if from below, unreasonable
and uncanny, so also God comes up at him or in at him, and
his response is the song of response. If he sings with Charlotte
Elliot (1789—1871):

> "Now to be thine, yea thine alone,
>   O Lamb of God I come"

he sings the song of sex, because this is the nearest equivalent
to his experience. To be in love is to be in song. To be in
God is to be in song also. "God moved", "the morning stars
sang". Man in the modern world responds with ever more
and more noise. "We have become so accustomed to living
with noise that many of us feel psychologically insecure
when we are left to ourselves with our thoughts."[5] Within
the homes of the industrial workers the "sound" of the box
is virtually never off, in work, in conversation, or in reading,
or during meals. Our age is the age of din—the din of
machinery, the thunder of warfare, the perpetual drone of
wireless and television. The man at his prayers must com-
pete, enter into the ever-increasing din of creation, and
offer his humble theme that it may be perceived despite the
drums of hell.

MUSIC AND PRODUCTIVITY

The labourer building a pyramid in ancient Egypt sang
together with his fellows to ease his burden. Not long ago
the stevedore in London Docks would sing to bring relief to
his day and to liven the work. Today the factory hand has
his sound artificially projected at him in "Music While You
Work".

The Church will do ill to take no notice of these things.
Wyatt and Langdon reported from the Medical Research
Council in 1937: "There were a few isolated instances in
which the music seemed to have little or no effect on individual production." In the industrial factories tested, "when

music was played the increase in output varied from 6.2%
to 11.3%." It is proved that man responds to artificial
sound in some measure as he responds to his own song. If
the industrial world requires for productivity the sound of
music, shall we not also suppose productivity of prayer may
require the same. May we be spared the artificial apparatus
in Church but let us note the wisdom of the commercial
tycoon.[6]

Wynford Reynolds, reporting on "Music While You
Work" for the B.B.C. in the middle of the war (1942),
found that rhythms and tempo do not affect working
speeds. It was the gaiety and cheerfulness which music can
inspire which aided war effort. It was not for nothing that
eight million war workers were found to be listening to
"Music While You Work". Thus the Church does well to
note that music still has the power to enliven man and it is a
fact that few indeed are immune to it.

THE WORLD OF HEALTH AND EDUCATION

If there are two common denominators of mankind in the
twentieth century, it would be hard to find any more
common than the hospital and the school. Wherever
Western European culture spreads it takes the hospital and
the school. The Indian, the African, the communist and the
capitalist all have in common the surgeon and the class-
room. Religion and creed divide the "one people". Culture
and dress divide the "one people". The hospital, the pill,
the blood transfusion, mathematics and the desire to read
unite mankind.

What has the Church made of this? The missionary will
reply: we gave them to the "one people". Did we not
produce the big London hospitals with their holy dedications
and also their training schools? Did we not produce
Oxbridge from the Dominican and Franciscan traditions?
Did we not give Africa and India their first foundation

schools and colleges? All this is true, but what effect has this had on the liturgical worship of the Church?

The use of music in the healing of disease is as old as Adam. Othello can say, " . . . an admirable musician! O, she will sing the savageness out of a bear." The daily offices of the Church are for the healing and wholeness of the "one people" of God, and we can no longer regard the nature of song as irrelevant. Even the dentist has discovered that music smoothes our delirium, prevents vomiting and ensures rapid emergence from the chair![7]

We know that musical sounds break up and dissolve cholesterol, and affect gallstones and blood vessels. Ira Altshuler in the *American Journal of Psychiatry* (1944) suggests that "one would expect a medium which affects emotion, the endocrines, the circulation, the respiration, the blood pressure, the mood, association and imagery, would be worthy of further (medical) investigation". Yet while the medical officer experiments to test and prove in modern scientific terms the therapeutic values of music, the Church, the "Singing Church", throws away its heritage and leaves the parish priest to bind up with his spattering of clinical theology the mentally sick and neurotic souls within his cure, whose numbers increase alarmingly year by year.

Nor must the Church wait to exploit the value of song until the soul is sick. Music has long been seen as an educational aid to forming a balanced personality. Music is an excellent diet for the young, for if infinite harmony does exist then indeed the young grow up *in harmonia* with being, true existential being—Christians simply say with God. Antagonisms and tensions diminish and the body is brought into harmony. The Greeks saw music as vital to education, to the development of character and the health of the body. Aristotle would have it that music is for (a) amusement, (b) education, (c) enjoyment and (d) purification. Now if Aristotle is correct in the fourth καθαρσις, how closely must music be related to the liturgy. "Almighty God, unto whom all hearts be open, all desires known, and from whom no secrets are hid; *cleanse* . . . "

For Plato, music is more than an art. The citizen "will also have to aim not at music which is pleasing but which is right".[8]

A more modern appraisement is found in *Music in the Life of Man* by Julius Portnoy. "Children find music extremely helpful as an aid in learning. Music aids in the education both of the mind and of the emotions. Music sharpens a child's sensibilities and familiarizes him with his emotional resources. Music intensifies his capacity to feel and probe. Music gives him a sense of order which the outside world does not supply. Music converts the animal in him and transforms him into an affectionate child, sublimates his feelings of hurt and revenge into love and devotion. Education is the sensitizing of the whole child, not of the mind alone."[9]

All the world wants education. All the world can sing. Those whose duty it is to reconstruct the liturgical prayers of the Church in the twentieth century must think in terms of the hospital and the school as well as in terms of devotion.

CHAPTER TWELVE

Theological Considerations in Liturgical Reform

THE TRAINING OF MEN IN PRAYER

We have every reason to hope that in the cathedral the office will be at its best and its finest. If the office grows apart in its essentials from that offered in the parishes, then immediately detachment and disunity in the dioceses must follow. In the early days of the conversion of England, men were trained in community under the bishop. They then went out on mission and did the office as the bishop did it. When Bishop Christopher Wordsworth (1807—1885) and others sought to refashion the theological training for the ministry in the nineteenth century a host of little training colleges grew up, many around the cathedrals. We have to face the fact that the worship in the cathedrals had sunk to such an appalling state of degradation that it was not always wise to let young men pray daily in them or be trained in them. In Lincoln, as in some other cathedral cities, an unhappy compromise was reached.

The effect of this compromise has been of untold harm to the strength of the Church in the twentieth century. Men have been trained in small houses with devotional private chapels, some under party colours. All the loyalties which the priest now attaches to his old college ought to attach him to his bishop, his cathedral and his teaching canons, and the mother Church.

"Now to Anglicans it is almost unthinkable that in a

community like a theological college or seminary the celebration of the Holy Communion should not be a frequent, if
not daily, event in its life. I remember," says Reginald
Fuller, "my surprise that this was not so in the Evangelisches
Stift at Tübingen in 1938-1939, and I got a very significant
explanation that the Lord's Supper was not an occasion for
a group like a seminary, but for a parochial congregation . . .
Since the Eucharist is essentially an activity of the whole
church in one place, it could be questioned whether a
specialized group ought to celebrate the Eucharist. At least
a right understanding of the liturgy should preclude its
doing so on a Sunday."[1] The solving of this devotional
problem may be done on the lines suggested in Dr. John
Robinson's "*The House Church and the Parish Church.*"[2] But this
is not our concern. The issue before us is that men in
training to be priests should have a right relationship in the
prayers and offices with authority and diocesan organisation
on the one hand, and with the *laos* on the other.

The clergy have so little sense of belonging together, or
doing a job together, because quite simply they, as a diocesan
team, have so seldom prayed together. Many talk about the
purpose of the cathedral in the twentieth century. A cathedral must be none other than the place where the bishop
and his staff pray. We ought to be quite clear that the cost
of maintaining a cathedral gives us honest return in terms
of mission and conversion. The Church is not a society for
the maintenance of national architecture or musical heir-
looms. A cathedral was not built because William Byrd's
Great Service would sound well in it, though this is the stage
we have almost reached. In the mid twentieth century,
evensong can be broadcast every week by the B.B.C. The
names of the musicians past and present are the only names
mentioned. We are not given the bishop or even the dean
leading the worship of a great church and diocese at prayer.
It is the cathedral musicians at work, and let us not be
unkind about this for we must face it squarely: the organists

of our great cathedrals are often better known than our
clergy. Our musicians have saved our cathedrals from being
solely architectural museum pieces. Dr. P. C. Moore has
suggested that laymen would make better cathedral
treasurers; perhaps it is time the organist had his place in
the chapter house.[3] Here we must see first what history has
to say about the office and the cathedral.

THE MUSICIAN DIVORCED

Every English choirboy knows that his choir must be divided
for liturgical worship into sides and these are "Decani" and
"Cantoris". The dean was, of course, the leader and ruler
of the church and so led one side of the antiphonal prayer.
The cantor sat at the head of the other side. He was second
in seniority. Dr. Kathleen Edwards makes it clear that the
cantor's (or precentor's) duty of ordering the prayers and
praises of the community was superior to any other duty in
the community.[4] There we touch the root of much failure.
The nature of worship is of the utmost importance to
mission. If the senior men of our cathedrals had been
intimately concerned with the singing of the office since the
Reformation we may be certain we should not now have an
office unrevised since 1662.

In the sixth century, cantors could be promoted to the
diaconate without ecclesiastical exams because they served
the sanctuary. Bede tells us that James, a Master of Song
at Canterbury, was raised to the See of York in 633. Music
in itself was, in the Aristotelian tradition, a part of learning.
Alcuin wrote in 796 to his old pupil Eanbald that education
was to be organised under grammar, song and writing. As
late as 1305, there could be a row in Lincoln because new
schools were teaching song and thereby depriving the
mother Church of her proper monopoly in the song school.

By the eleventh century things were beginning to go
wrong. In the monasteries men were beginning to be chosen

9

as precentor for their ability in learning and as directors of studies, though they continued to exercise oversight also over the *opus Dei*. We see the pattern develop. Music becomes no longer the concern of the highest authority over the whole house: it gradually becomes the concern of a lesser man. It tends to become a specialist activity. Extensive singing in harmony or in parts begins and of this "abusive chanting" Roger Bacon complains most bitterly in 1267.[5] (cf. page 113). The interested or musically agile go off at a tangent. The organ starts its steady damming up the human voice of praise. The organist appears round about the twelfth century. By 1463, he is playing daily at the mass of the Blessed Virgin Mary at Salisbury.

Nevertheless Byrd at Lincoln and Tallis at Waltham and others like them were very much part of the praying community when the first edition of Common Prayer was published. They are essentially ecclesiastics, part of the body corporate, not laymen paid by a small caucus of canons to "do" for them. In 1616 at Chichester it became necessary to tell the organist that if he was not playing he ought to be downstairs taking his part in the singing of the office. On December 18th 1660 the chapter at Westminster found it necessary to order the organ loft door to be shut and to tell the organist, Christopher Gibbons, to put on "his surplice and betake himself to his stall".[6] Hence he is already on the way to being a mechanic or technician rather than a monk. The present organist of Westminster Abbey might be a little shocked if he was detailed regularly to sing the epistle as Orlando Gibbons, his predecessor, used to do at the Chapel Royal.[7] We find in the early reformed era a number of musicians still following the old tradition. John Merbecke (d. 1585) was more interested in his concordance than in his compositions. Christopher Tye (1497-1573) was ordained priest and took orders in 1560 and was given a living near Ely.

As time goes on the parting of the ways between clerk in

holy orders and lay clerk in the Daily Praise becomes wider and wider. Little chinks of light show through as when "the Elect of Chichester . . . betook himself to sing the Litany, the choir answering" at Archbishop Parker's consecration on December 17th 1559 in Lambeth Palace.[8] Or again Williams, Bishop of Lincoln, observed the offices "noon and evening, with music . . . the Bishop himself bearing the tenor part *among them* often". But by the time we come to the twentieth century there has been a total divorce between priest and layman, a nominal place in the leading of praise being given to a minor canon but the actual directing of the praise of God being (in reality if not in name) so much in the hands of the lay musician. The latter finds himself *de facto* responsible for keeping going that for which the cathedral was built, but at the same time he finds himself a mere paid servant rather than a "corporate member of the Chapter".

THE CATHEDRAL CANON IN THE TWENTIETH CENTURY

The first half of the twentieth century saw a high water mark in cathedral worship, a generation of often scholarly deans and canons supported invariably by musicians who were sound churchmen. Choirs were better than a century before. Musical standards had gone up and up. Dr. Fellows at Windsor (a minor canon of the old school, who held on later than most to the medieval rights of petty canons) was able in a long ministry there to refurnish the cathedrals with Elizabethan music and so enable them to return to some of their former glory. The rendering of some of this music has reached a higher standard of performance in some churches than its composers probably dreamed of. The beauty of worship was to sound out again—sheer sound as not heard for centuries or possibly ever before. This was good, but neither church nor cathedral can live only on the past.

The canons of the mid twentieth century are far less often in their choir than were the canons of the 1930s. The age of the motor car is also the age of diocesan utility canons. Absenteeism caused by pluralities of former generations has been fought and won. The cathedral dean now suffers from efficiency absenteeism—men who are too engaged by the speed of development of the post-industrial age to give honest time daily to the cathedral office as it ambles its pedestrian way to the New Jerusalem. In recent years I heard in an organ loft the minor canon begin his penitential sentences for evensong. I saw an old cathedral organist leave his stool day by day and look over the top to see which of the residentiaries were present, and then he would return to his stool with a sense of hunger. His work, after all, was to help the chapter pray. Where were the chapter? In too much hurry with their correspondence to spare so long a time for an office? Or were they being too efficient here and there in the diocese?

THE THEOLOGY OF THE CATHEDRAL CHURCH IN THE TWENTIETH CENTURY

It would be out of place in the context of this book to examine the causes of decline in daily cathedral attendances at the daily offices in the last thirty years. What we can justly ask is what effect ought the ecumenical movement to be having on the daily office in the cathedral? The Provost of Coventry, writing on *The Twentieth Century Cathedral* is probably wide of the mark when he sees the pre-Reformation cathedral as a "great centre of experimental creative activity".[9]

The great Gothic creations of Canterbury, Lincoln and Lichfield as they stand today were built as glorified chantries where prayer was made for souls departed. The giving of the buildings was part of the payment for salvation, and the theological collapse of the doctrine of merit underlies the collapse of the corporate human body essential to the stones. Glastonbury and Tintern disappeared, others survived as utility cathedrals to help govern a national Church and keep the commonwealth in shape; but they are like Ichabod —the glory is departed. The theological character of the twentieth century is the character of ecumenicity, of unity, of withdrawal for action, for mission. The theological climate is heated up by the world environment of inter-racial tension and continental onslaught.

The cathedral office, therefore, in the twentieth century will have consciously to leave behind something of the chantry in its daily prayer in order to make room for: (a) the withdrawal of the faithful remnant into pentecostal prayer; the clutching up of fire behind closed doors; the gathering of the will in small communion to face mission in the streets and market places of the city, and on the shop floor of the works or in the seats of scientific learning; (b) the drawing into prayer of those who pass by in this age of Jehu, when everybody is going faster than everybody else to somewhere more urgently, when tourists and businessmen pass in or out of the cathedral doors as pilgrims on a scale hitherto undreamt of. As Dr. Moore has said: "If the vergers are to the tourists what the air hostesses are to the holiday-makers—something seems to have gone radically wrong."[10] The cathedral office (like the parochial daily office) need not necessarily be understood by the man in the pew who is passing by, but it must seem to him to be intelligent. He cannot expect to fathom the depths of the Church's experience in a flash, but it must not offend his mentality. If it is genuine, it will draw him as a magnet, as Jesus drew the people. At present one can see so often before evensong begins the multitudes who could perhaps have followed Christ being excluded from the doors because it is "service time". I have sat at the back of a transept and watched those who were not used to such things stay to see; then one by one get up and leave, till when the State prayers were said there remained those few only, who came intentionally to be at evensong that day. There was no magnetism there to hold them for even forty minutes. Sightseers are not rushed for time.

THE LITURGICAL POSSIBILITIES IN THE TWENTIETH CENTURY

(a) The Introduction

Now it is easy, of course, to postulate that the cathedral must be an inner fire of the spirit and also a house of missionary evangelism. It is less easy to see what kind of liturgy could ever fill this bill. Let us look first at evensong for this has become, thanks to the musicians, the part of the cathedral cake most often consumed.

Let the archdeacon or canon ask himself: "When I was a lone parish priest with my own small church, did I say daily the whole introduction of the Protestant reform of 1552? Did I day by day find it real to work carefully through the confession and to repeat twice the Lord's Prayer?" If it was no use to him then, it is no use to him now; even though he has interested a minor canon to do it for him, who has the gift of making it sound beautiful, and true, and as if he has never said it before. The canon's prayer must be natural in his cathedral. Because there is a crowd it does not change the necessary ingredients. Most of us find that the introduction as a twice daily menu will not digest, and in any case it is a mistake psychologically. It is unsound then to force it on to the choristers and others in the cathedral daily.

The psalmody we have dealt with at length already. The lessons fall beyond the scope of this book, except to note that they are invariably well read today and listened to with more appreciation than most of the service. "He who 'in the spirit' reads the written word lives in the numinous, though he may have neither notion of it nor name for it, nay, though he may be unable to analyse any feeling of his own and so make explicit to himself the nature of that numinous strand running through the religious experience."[11]

(b) The Evening Canticles

I doubt if the *Magnificat* sung daily as the centre climax of the office is typical of Anglican theological opinion of the mid twentieth century. I must not here judge what part Our Lady plays in modern thinking and the prayer of congregations, only say that if the residentiary's writings and sermons do not reflect this teaching then the *Magnificat* daily is dead wood. There is no doubt whatever that the thinking man in the pew has considerable difficulty with it. Beginning with the quite ridiculous word (in this context) "magnify" it goes on, "For behold, from henceforth: all generations shall call me blessed", which to him is un-Christlike or thorough "swank". Amongst the difficulties is the one about the rich being sent empty away, which in this affluent age is a hard blow to most of the congregations of the Province of Canterbury, if not so much of York. Perhaps, as with Taizé and the monks of Berne, some variation in canticles is a possibility. Frere reminded us of the daily medieval variations and suggested the use of hymns, such as the φως ἱλαρον.[12]

The *Nunc Dimittis* causes less concern, and does well if used as Cranmer intended as the final song before going off for the evening and to bed. Rounded off by the evening collects and a little silence and a quiet departure, as in vespers, all is well. For us it has lost reality first by the introduction of an anthem in "Quires and Places" but much worse by the recitations for the Royalty. The parish church often finds the vicar catching up with the T.V. News in a spattering of collects. If the *Nunc Dimittis* and the evening collects are to remain then they certainly ought to be at the end of the office.

(c) The Anthem

The anthems would probably serve best as an adjunct to the psalms or the first lesson or the second lesson. It can be shown that the first anthems for English words written subsequent to the 1549 Prayer Book were invariably prayers.

The composers understood "the anthem" in that period as
an appendage to the third collect and treated it as a choral
prayer. They developed only the simple motet form similar
to the Latin use.

The Elizabethan and Caroline composers allowed themselves a far greater liberty with the appointed order of
service than we would accept today. Almost all their work
was the setting to song of words within the prescribed
liturgical forms. It was very rarely that the words of an
anthem were not part of the liturgical prayer of the day.
They were thoroughly relevant to the theme of the particular
worship. The setting of the entire collect was a regular form;
for example, John Mudd (cf. note 14, ch. 12) does out
beautifully the collect for the Tenth Sunday after Trinity,
"Let thy merciful ears, O Lord". Orlando Gibbons (1583–
1625) was organist of Westminster and associated with
the worship there from 1604 to 1625. It can be shown
that of all his anthems which survive, hardly any are
haphazard writings but each was composed for a particular
liturgical and theological purpose. The modern cathedral
organist aspires towards this. In practice we have to admit
his anthem invariably ends by being simply "a piece". The
pre-Commonwealth musicians enjoyed setting the English
liturgy to music. It was liturgy and not simply good music
offered as the choir's offering.[13]

In 1663 James Clifford published a list of works of
anthems commonly sung. Of a hundred and sixty-seven
anthems, almost half were set to words of psalms and in
many cases were complete psalms clearly used within the
office and the eucharist. Of the remainder, almost fifty
represent complete prayers or collects. This illustrates what
I said earlier. The earliest English composers, working with
the Book of Common Prayer, treated the anthem as an
extension of the third collect or else turned parts of the
liturgy into anthem form. Since no less than twenty-one of
these are collects from the Prayer Book it is not at all im-

probable that they were sometimes sung by the choir instead of by the minor canon at the normal place for the collect in the office.[14]

The composers felt very free at this period to adopt and abbreviate and adapt the Prayer Book and its rubrics. Adherence to the letter of the law in the printed word had not yet come in. Orlando Gibbons can set to work to do his psalms for the glorious Feast of Pentecost. He finds in his 1552 book the propers set as 104 and 145. He makes no pretence at trying to do the impossible, that is to "pray" both of the two. He selects Psalm 145. He then begins it entirely on his own initiative with verse 15: "The eyes of all wait upon thee, O Lord". He thoroughly catches the vision of the apostolic company gathered in wait upon the Spirit, works his way through seven verses and ends at 21 with a splash on "all flesh give thanks", in the feeling of the context of the fulfilment of Joel. This is loyalty to the Prayer Book with a pre-1662 difference.

William Byrd of Lincoln Minster was disgusted with the massacre of the mass. He no doubt felt that if they had to end abruptly at the intercession with those collects at the end it should be done as decently as possible, and so got to work with a full choral version of "Prevent us O Lord", a collect set apart in 1549 under that unhappy rubric "Collects to be said after the offertory, when there is no Communion, every such day one". Dr. Tye (1497-1572) at Ely, already bored with the endless *Nunc Dimittis*, writes a full Psalm 67 to be sung in place of *Nunc Dimittis* as allowed in the 1552 Prayer Book.

Of all the hundred and sixty-seven anthems in Clifford's Restoration period volume, sixteen only are from the New Testament. Three only are Old Testament (omitting Psalms). Thus we have more than sixty of them psalms, almost fifty collects and prayers and merely twenty Bible texts.

How markedly the whole situation got completely out of

hand with the Restoration. The anthem became part of the entertainment in the Chapel Royal. Henry Purcell (1659-1695) writes a beautiful work "My Beloved Spake". It serves as a good illustration of the direction church music was to take, a blind alley from which composers such as Walmesley and Stanford tried to lead us out more than two hundred years later.

> "My beloved spake, and said unto me,
> Rise up, my love, my fair one, and come away.
> For, lo, the winter is passed, the rain is over and gone;
> The flowers appear on the earth;
> The time of the singing of birds is come . . .
>
> Rise up, my love, my fair one, and come away . . .
> My beloved is mine, and I am his.
>
> (Song of Sol. 2. 10f.)

To the medieval liturgist this had served as a good allegory of Christ and his Church. To the Restoration congregation it was a jolly good ecclesiastical echo of the debauched court at St. James where Purcell had been a choirboy.

The extended use of Old Testament for anthems became the play game of the eighteenth century and nineteenth century. This vast range of literature gave endless scope for "spot me and write one". Cranmer must turn in his grave on hearing his evening collects of the night followed by, for example, the Cantata of Sir John Goss (1800-1880), containing the whole of chapter 35 of Isaiah—the wilderness and the solitary place with the feeble, the fearful heart, the ears of the deaf, the eyes of the blind, lion and ravenous beasts and all. Cranmer wanted you to sleep after evensong, not dream!

The number of twentieth-century composers who find it necessary now to choose ye olde englishe text for the anthems simply shows the total stupidity which surrounds so much writing of church music.

"Most glorious Lord of lyfe! that, on this day,
Did'st make thy triumph over death and sin;
And, having harrow'd hell, did'st bring away
Captivity thence captive, us to win:
This joyous day, deare Lord, with joy begin;
And grant that we, for whom thou did'st dye,
Being with thy deare blood clene washt from sin,
May live for ever in filicity!
And that thy love we weighing worthily,
May likewise love thee for the same again;
And for thy sake, that all lyke deare did'st buy,
With love may one another entertayne!
So let us love, deare Love, lyke as we ought:
Love is the lesson which the Lord us taught."[15]

This style of thing is common. Edmund Spenser's English is beautiful but just what has this to do with theology or the mission of the Church to industrial England in the twentieth century?

So, if it was intended that "in quires and places where they sing" an anthem should follow, it was intended that it be something of the fashion of the pre-Prayer Book Latin motet and this is how the earlier composers treated it. The pre-Restoration use of prayers was the obvious treatment and it was no doubt rounded off with the Grace, and so to bed.

(d) *Liturgical Prayer in the Office*

If it is felt that some scope must be given to confession and intercession within the office, then surely the place for this is after the Creed. Some time could be given for penitence following the shorter *Kyrie*. A thrice daily absolution is unfitted to the twentieth century since Sigmund Freud watered down so much good sin.

The *Kyrie* would be much better in its ancient form. Jungmann has shown us that a threefold *Kyrie* was invented in the ninth century when people had forgotten that the

word "*Kyrie*" in the litany meant Christ. There is little need
now for us to keep up with the repercussions of Teutonic
Arianism or go on singing threefold *Kyries*.[16] On the contrary, mock Trinitarian theology pushed down our necks
day after day robs the liturgy of the Holy Spirit and Moving
Fire of the Church.

This would make an intelligent pattern: a *Kyrie*, followed
by a penitence (a silence with or without an alternative
liturgical form), followed by the Lord's Prayer and an intercession (another silence with or without an alternative
liturgical form). Then we must bear in mind that the
responses follow much the same order of intercession as
"the Prayer for the whole state of Christ's Church" in the
eucharist.[17] They suitably gather up the community intercession to one mind for the final rendering of the collect.
The collects then will gather up the prayers of all within the
Church's liturgy.

Addleshaw tells us that the idea that "the office ends with
the third Collect finds no support in the thought of the
seventeenth century". The liturgists of the period, he says,
all speak of the office ending with what we term the State
Prayers. He goes on to claim that "The anthem or psalm
served the double purpose of marking the division between
petitionary and intercessionary prayer and preventing the
congregation finding the prayers too long".[18]

This seems to me to be argument derived from the pious
murmurings of loyal churchmen of the seventeenth century
who tried to justify the anomaly. Did not Cranmer intend
the offices to end with the final third collects. Both of these
send one off into action: on the one hand "neither run into
any kind of danger" as you go off across the road running
for the bus or meeting up with the office girl; or on the
other "defend us from all perils", bad dreams or goblins
as we go to bed.

These 1662 State prayers first made their appearance in
the Scottish Book of 1637. The theological opinions of

Archbishop Laud are well stated there. In the years immediately prior to the murder of the sovereign and the Archbishop of Canterbury, it is not surprising that additional intercessions should have been advisable for those persons and those pertaining to them. We might well call them regulations in time of "national emergency". It could also be maintained that even in 1662 there was still revolution in the air. For us to continue to unbalance the office Cranmer so carefully planned won't do either. The "national emergency" which necessitated these prayers is past and to continue to use them now, more than three hundred years after it is all over, is typical of what happens in affairs liturgical.

(e) *Mattins*

So far as mattins is concerned we are on simple ground. Canons at Westminster found it necessary to sing mattins at 8 a.m. in 1549. On Saturdays they went off afterwards to the Chapter House where the chanter reported the attendance weekly of singing men *and* prebendaries. Prebendaries absent were charged 2s. for the common fund.[19] It seems to be unreasonable to expect everybody to down tools at 10 a.m. as at present at St. Paul's, Westminster, and most English provincial cathedrals. The result of this eccentricity is that St. Michael's, Tenbury, is almost the only place in England left where you can hear mattins regularly and properly sung. (They sing their office at 8.45.)

The Book of Common Prayer is so much a product of the Benedictine system that the notion of mattins as a high morning service just does not fit. Mattins must be a morning office—a day's beginning. The psalms as described in chapter ten are only meaningful this way. To say in front of a handful of visiting tourists at 10.45 a.m. "who has safely brought us to the beginning of this day" is telling the world that the Church is regulated to the routine of old maids who take poodles out in the park after coffee in bed at nine.

We take far too little account of the fact that people can

now read for themselves. In mattins it might well be better to have a period for reading in which the clergy can use the time to meditate and study to prepare background material for the perpetual pouring forth of the word which the Reformation has forced upon us. Benedictine monks of the fifteenth century needed to be read to as a community. We need to be in community, but this does not necessitate our being read to six times a day.

The *Te Deum* is something obviously for high days. How much better we should appreciate *Benedictus* if it took its turn with the others. The monks of Berne in their *Little Breviary* suggest various alternative canticles, as also does Harold Riley in his *Revision of the Psalter*. These may be gathered up from the ancient tradition of Codex Alexandrinus (fifth century) which contains fourteen canticles, among which we find a *Gloria in Excelsis, Magnificat, Nunc Dimittis* and *Benedictus*. The greater part of these fourteen became the nine odes of "Orthros" (c. 550 A.D.). Our experience of canticle has now ceased to be "the singing Bible", partly through the rude intrusion of psalm alternatives in 1552, and partly through the lack of variety which causes a feeling of formality rather than song.

The morning office must then be something communal. It is "us" after all. "O come, let *us* sing . . . let *us* come before his presence." The presence doesn't mean to come and bow deeply before a particular altar table or in a particular Church. It means the presence must be there in the new day, new life, the sun again, the being again, the being, with being, in being. After all, God woke up first unless you saw the sun rise (if you are a Psalter Christian). The presence of God is the light of day, not that molten image in wood and stone.

The reader may be worrying about the visitors in and about the cathedral at the hour of morning coffee. There is nothing more joyous than to find a cathedral alive when you enter. If this is important then no doubt there is something that can be done about it. Some kind of worship and reading of the word is obviously what could be expressed here. But mattins is in its place and time a vehicle of beauty for a community and should not be unobligingly lodged upon mid-morning visitors.

The form of mattins should be shaped around the community. Where there is a school or collegiate body obviously dean and boy ought to pray together.

One is reminded of Lancelot Andrewes when he took schoolboys out two by two walking down the Thames bank in the afternoons, when Dean of Westminster. He not only prayed with his boys but according to John Hackett, who was a boy when Andrewes was Dean, he actually took over the duties of headmaster and usher for a week at a time "and gave us not an hour of loitering time from morning to night".[20] Constitutionally the school consisted of dean, twelve prebendaries, two masters and forty scholars. Constitutionally Church and school were one. At that stage organically they were one. The final rupture took place after the Public Schools Act, 1868.[21] Recently we have had Dr. P. C. Moore pleading in *English Church Music 1965* for a revival of the educational responsibilities of the greater churches, and even posing the question of sex in cathedral constitutions. For a century now we have educated our women. The cathedral is still a male closed shop.

Not all cathedral establishments may be able to rekindle the educational light. There must however surely be in this age of Parkinson's Law an office staff and episcopal administration. In such cases ought not the mattins to be something that both the bishop and his shorthand typist can share?

CHAPTER THIRTEEN

Concerning "Common Prayer"

"For there are many superfluities which beget weariness
rather than devotion, both to hearers, and to officiants; as
for instance, at Prime on Sundays, when Priests have to say
three Masses and the people await them, yet there is none
to celebrate, for they are yet busied with Prime. So also with
the recitation of the eighteen Psalms at Nocturns on Sunday
before the *Te Deum*. For these things beget sheer weariness,
not only in summer, when we are harassed by fleas and the
nights are short and the heat is intense, but in winter also.
There are yet many things left in divine service which might
be changed for the better. And it would be well if they were
changed, for they are full of uncouth stuff, though not every
man can see this."[1]

They were full of uncouth stuff indeed. The medieval
layman certainly spoke his mind "plain". Despite the Book
of Common Prayer the layman still sometimes watches his
parish priest getting through mattins alone, before he starts
the parish communion. There is still "sheer weariness" and
still "not every man can see" that things "might be changed
for the better".

THE DAILY OFFICE AND THE COMMUNITY

In the last chapter we were concerned with the cathedral.
It was, however, for the parish church that the Book of
Common Prayer was made. Martin Thornton reminds us

that the Book was framed to do for the parish what the Benedictine *Regula* had done for the monastery. Both the *Regula* and the Book of Common Prayer are designed "for an integrated and united community *predominantly lay*".[2]

Many contemporary clergy have been brought up on an ascetical discipline which encouraged them to think of the office as "the priest's daily office". The prayer they were to offer on behalf of their people was a private individualistic devotion. Whilst being careful not to deny that this discipline has done much to preserve the sanctity of both priest and parish, the historical fact is that this is not what was intended by the Book of Common Prayer, for the latter is full of choruses, such as *Te Deum* daily, and dialogues such as responses and psalmody. The 1549 Preface reads "that the people by daily hearing . . . " etc., etc.

It is not intelligent to use the binary form of Hebrew psalmody in public worship in any other way than in two voices. "The bi-partite structure of the verse . . . demands an antiphonal rendering."[3] Thus when a psalm is sung through "full" by a choir inevitably the pattern is missed, as one would miss the sense of a dialogue in Shakespeare if it was all read in one tone.

There are those who think of this formality, this Benedictine ordering of things, as a lost cause in a "world come of age". The daily office with the eucharist is in fact the "existential act of the Body of Christ". The conduct of the daily prayer of the Church is not an optional good work but "the ontological unity of the divine organism".[4] Any reform of the office which would follow Dr. Hunter (cf. p. 93) and make Sunday mattins and evensong a special show is only adding fuel to the fire for those who see these things as at best unessential to belief: voluntary extras, if you care for that sort of thing.

At the parish level the only theology of church-going that will survive will be the theology of a perpetually recollected Life, continuing in and through the increasingly secular society. Only when we have got people back to offering their Common Prayer in their homes and knowing it as Common Prayer, will they see again the joy of being able to do this thing together. To attempt to make the daily offices a Sunday "do" is asking for them to be ignored. "For the Christians of antiquity, the liturgy was not a school of prayer, or the school of prayer, but it was their prayer."[5]

THE DAILY OFFICE AND THE LAYMAN

In a little book *The Work of God* (1965) a religious of the C.S.M.V. asks if the Jewish custom of the *Ma'amed* could not be introduced in the parishes, that is, if a small company of laity could not be recruited to take it in turns to join in the daily office.[6] There would be little difficulty in bringing this about, certainly in the evenings, if the office could be made alive. One is mindful that the Jews in their prayers on ordinary days did not have lections.[7] Our ordering of psalmody and lectionary as they stand make this unreasonable. The same writer pleads that we have got to recapture "the vision of the Work of God" (the daily office) and show again that it is "the privilege and duty of every Christian, in some form or measure". To be a Christian is to have part in this experience, to be branch to the vine.

We have learned to expect in many countries a decreasing number of ordinands. It was the Bishop of Posadas in Argentina who, at the recent Vatican Council, pressed for liturgical provision for priestless congregations. We have in England ever-growing parishes with an increasing rate of mental disorder which calls for pastoral care. The rate of physical breakdown amongst the English clergy in some places is now alarmingly high. The daily office should be conducted by the laity. In these days when most can read there is no reason whatever why a clerk in holy orders needs to be present. In many parts of my parish in Africa there were churches in which I had personally never led a daily office, but prayer was always made in them. It was one dark night when I searched for my African fellow priest in church that I learned what the daily office was about. I found no priest, there was only a young man singing his heart out at the far end. "He had to go," he said, "so I am here."

What is done in the daily office must needs be done in little more than fifteen minutes. What is done must be acceptable to the manual worker who doesn't read *The Times* nor care for theological or typological debate. He can and will find his home, his feelings, and the injustices of the world as he sees it, in the psalms. He will also find there the wherewithal of praise. "The basic motive for our use of the Psalter as our fundamental prayer" is because it is "the Prayer of Man" and "the Word of God" at the same time.[8]

As there are many parts to the body of Christ and we are not all called to one office or administration, so in liturgy we do not all have the same offering to make. Bouyer sees the Church as necessarily a hierarchial organisation resulting from the apostolicity of the Church. So in the daily office the parish priest has no special part to play unless it be the absolution, teaching or the dismissal.

This author also reminds us that frequently prime and compline have displaced lauds and vespers: a sentimental appeal to our preoccupation with work and sleep is stronger than the appeal of the praise of God.

It is no good trying to continue to put "God in the gaps"; to have snippets of prayer before and after little meetings to sanctify them, to have holy sessions for confirmation candidates of which the Caroline divines would never have approved, and to slap hymns on the entertainment surfaces. "Veneers of religion will not count for the conversion of England. The *Regula* and the Daily Office remain 'the solid anchor' in a world of anxiety . . . "[9]

The manual worker and the down-town clerk can recognise the Word of God and it can touch him. He can sing a song. Contrary to much popular opinion, he can clothe himself with fine literary forms of prayer. These then are what Cranmer wanted him to have, and which we saw, in chapters seven and eight, slowly and artlessly frozen to death.

Do not expect this man now to grow rich in a week. Again we must be reminded, "No one can sing the psalms who does not know them by heart. All he can be expected to do is to follow."[10] We are going to have very humble beginnings if the "Singing Church" in its little parishes up and down the land is to sing again the praise of God. The singing of the praise of God is coincidentally also the first priority in the principles of mission. The Book of Common Prayer is the people's book of praise. The scholar, the priest, and the religious orders have other aids to assist their devotions.

THE DAILY OFFICE IN SOLITUDE

All that has been said of the office being both a lay and a communal activity, does not prohibit us from asking: "What of the lone priest or the woman who cannot leave her babes at home?"

The Archbishop of Canterbury has warned us in his *Durham Essays and Addresses* to be careful to think on parish communions and not to suppose a crowd becomes a community. A gathering does not presuppose either unity or spirituality.[11] "The Christian at prayer is never alone and need never feel himself to be alone." Rupert E. Davies (a Baptist) goes on, "His togetherness with the whole Church should never be simply implicit . . . it should come out in the way he prays and the method he uses.

"Has the time not come," Davies asks, "when we may contemplate the drawing up of Daily Offices which could be used by members—families—individuals of *all* traditions and all communions? They would be of real assistance to many individual Christians who wished to pray with the Church and they would help to bring Christians whose communions are still separated from each other into a real and growing unity."[12]

We need to get people away from thinking that to do an office they will need, if not a prie-dieu, at least a holy corner and a bed to kneel at. The Synagogue and the early Church both stood to pray. Much less kneeling was done in church before seats were put in to hide behind. We may well ask why the faithful get to their knees for the Lord's Prayer when we hear Mark 11. 25, "And when ye stand praying . . . forgive". Many will find the whole custom of standing easier at home. To be at a window or in a garden may well do more to help true contemplation with the Lord than smelling the eiderdown. But again to others, hands over the eyes induces a most valued relaxation and enables the resting of the mind. A wise monk wrote recently, "In order to benefit from the Offices we need ample relaxation . . . "[13]

Helene Lubienska de Lenval in *The Whole Man at Worship* wants us to be much more ready to let man pray with the limbs as well as the voice. "Actions express man at his deepest level". "How necessary it is for us to learn once more to pray with the body if we are to enter into the fulness of liturgical worship." Actions in prayer should always be traditional and habitual and taken out of use as soon as they become artificial. In these days we find many put their hands with palm to palm to pray. This was entirely unknown in the early Church and could have come from the Muslim east to the west via the court of Charlemagne. It lives still in feudal ceremonial and in the University of Cambridge when taking a degree. In the east we see it regularly as a courteous greeting. We must watch lest piety divorced from daily life produces greenhouse Christians.[14]

Addleshaw remarks that "The unity of man's nature, the interaction of body and spirit, give to all liturgical actions a peculiar importance." He continues, "Bodily actions become a real help to worship and make it easier for the faithful to take a full share in the service. It was a grasp of this unity which made the seventeenth-century liturgists lay emphasis on such ceremonies as kneeling for communion, bowing to the altar and at the name of Jesus, turning to the east for the gospel and Creed."[15]

The outward liturgical actions done in solitude must include the standing for praise. "Now therefore you may see plainly," says William Law, "the reason and necessity of singing of psalms; it is because outward actions are necessary to support inward tempers; and therefore the outward act of joy is necessary to raise and support the inward joy of the mind." Advocating hard the singing of psalms in daily private prayers, Law regards it as just as necessary as saying prayers. "You may as well think that you can be devout as you ought, without the use of prayer, as that you can rejoice in God as you ought, without the practice of singing psalms: because this singing is as much the natural language of praise and thanksgiving, as prayer is the natural language of devotion. I do not mean, that you should read over a psalm, but that you should chant or sing one of those psalms, which we commonly call the reading psalms. For singing is as much the proper use of a psalm as devout supplication is the proper use of a form of prayer: and a psalm only read is very much like a prayer that is only looked over." Furthermore, for those who do not cast themselves in the role of Christians standing privately in the bedroom proclaiming at the top of their voices the *Venite*, William Law points out, "If a person was to forbear praying, because he had an odd tone in his voice, he would have as good an excuse as he has, that forbears from singing psalms, because he has but little management of his voice. And as a man's speaking his prayers, though in an odd tone, may yet sufficiently answer all the ends of his own devotion; so a man's singing of a psalm, though not in a very musical way, may yet sufficiently answer all the ends of rejoicing in, and praising God. All men therefore are singers, in the same manner as all men think, speak, laugh, and lament."[16]

ONE PEOPLE, ONE CHURCH, ONE SONG

Let us take now, after many criticisms, two appraisals of the daily office, the first from a Congregationalist (J. S. Moffat) writing of Uganda more than half a century ago.

"In the Cathedral we joined in the stately service of the Anglican Church, never so stately and impressive as when it is rendered in noble simplicity, free from the adventitious accompaniment and vicarious performance of a highly trained choir. There was something more real and solemn than this in the vast murmur, almost a thunder-roll, of thousands of responding voices, the voices of men and women who had been born in the most degraded heathenism, the people that sat in darkness, but had seen a great light . . . (It was Easter Day.)[17]

Our second appraisal comes from a Roman Catholic whom we have often quoted, Louis Bouyer; he wrote quite recently:

"We must admit frankly that the offices of Morning Prayer and of Evensong as they are performed today in St. Paul's, Westminster Abbey, or York Minster or Canterbury Cathedral are not only the most impressive, but also one of the purest forms of Christian common prayer to be found anywhere in the world."[18]

We live in days when the Psalter is under attack from within the Church. It is despised as unsuitable for us in our sophisticated age, and to many more it is nothing but an imposition and a bore.

It holds for us the song of the soul, as well as the unity of the Church. The musicians may well have to think again if those who are "planted in the house of the Lord" (Ps. 92. 12) are to go out singing these songs on the factory floor. But the "Singing Church" will sing again. The songs will be the "One Song" of David. As they are sung beyond the barriers of historical divisions they will be sung by "One Church" till, in the words of Psalm 22 (appointed in the Common

Prayer for Good Friday), "all the ends of the world shall remember themselves, and be turned unto the Lord: and all the kindreds of the nations shall worship before him" as "one people".

"For the kingdom is the Lord's."

APPENDIX

A TABLE OF PSALMS
ARRANGED
FOR COMMON PRAYER

PSALMS AT MATTINS

Note

Below the psalm title are quoted the ancient or modern authorities who have used the psalm in a daily morning or evening prayer. Below that is a "pivot" or antiphon verse which may have suggested this use.

Abbreviations

G   Gregorian use
E   Eastern use
P   Parisian use
Q   Quignon's Breviary
LB *The Little Breviary*

Day	Psalm	Title
I	I	"The Two Ways" Q and LB Mattins (Sunday) v. 2 "exercise himself day and night"
2	2	"The Easter Psalm" Q Prime; LB Mattins (Sunday) v. 7 "this day have I begotten thee" (Resurrection Morning)
3	5	"For Morning Prayer" E Prime v. 3 "early in the morning will I . . . look up"
4	17	"A Prayer of David" E Terce; P Lauds; Q Prime (Tuesday) v. 3 "Thou hast in the night—season" visited my heart
5	19	"Λ Psalm of Heaven" E Orthros (daily) v. 5 "the sun . . . cometh forth"

Day	Psalm	Title

6   20   "A Prayer for the King"
E Orthros
v. 1 "The Lord hear thee in the day of trouble"

7   23   "A Psalm on the Shepherd"
G Prime (Sunday)
v. 2 "He shall . . . lead me forth"

8   25   "A Prayer for Forgiveness"
E Terce; G and Q Prime
v. 4 "Lead me forth"

9   30   "A Thanksgiving after Sickness"
G and LB Mattins; E Mesorion of Terce
v. 5 "joy cometh in the morning"

10   46   "The Might of God"
G Mattins; E Mesorion of Prime
v. 7 "The Lord of hosts is with us . . . "
(as we go to work)

11   50   "The Great Trial"
G Mattins
v. 1 "called the world, from the rising up of the sun"

12   54   "A Prayer for Deliverance"
G and Q Prime
v. 3 "For strangers are risen up against me . . . " (in daily life)

13   61   "A Royal Prayer"
G Mattins
v. 8 "that I may daily perform my vows"

14   62   "A Psalm of Quietness"
G Mattins
v. 10 "if riches increase . . . "
(through daily work)

Day	Psalm	*Title*
15	63	"A Royal Morning Prayer"

G Lauds; Q Prime (Chrysostom and Apostolic Constitutions)
v. 1 "early will I seek thee"

| 16 | 66 | "A Joyful Song" |

G Mattins; Q Lauds; P Mattins (Sunday)
v. 4 and 14 "O come and see"; "O come and hear" (Sunday Morning Worship)

| 17 | 67 | "The Candlestick Psalm" |

G Lauds; Q Prime
v. 2 "That thy way may be known upon earth . . . " (today as we Christians go about our duties)

| 18 | 90 | "The Funeral Psalm" |

E Prime; LB Lauds
v. 12 "So teach us to number our days"

| 19 | 92 | "A Song of the Sabbath" |

E Mesorion of Prime; G and LB Lauds
v. 2 "To tell of thy lovingkindness early in the morning"

| 20 | 93 | "The Clothing of God" |

E Mesorion of Prime; G Lauds (Sunday)
v. 1 "The Lord is King, and hath put on glorious apparel" (the dawn of creation)

| 21 | 94 | "A Prayer of Right Judgement" |

G Mattins; LB Mattins
v. 2 "Arise, thou Judge of the world"

| 22 | 95 | "The *Venite*" |

G Mattins
v. 8 "To-day, if ye will hear his voice"

Day	Psalm	Title
23	96	"God Comes to Judge" LB Lauds v. 2 "Tell ... his salvation from day to day"
24	97	"The Lord is King" G Mattins; LB Lauds v. 11 "There is sprung up a light"
25	100	"The *Jubilate*" G Mattins v. 3 "O go your way"
26	101	"The Accession Psalm" E Prime v. 9 "Every morning will I destroy" . . . (*Revised Psalter* 1963)
27	107	"For Those in Peril" G, Q and P Mattins v. 23 "They that go down to the sea in ships . . . " (and others to work elsewhere)
28	148	"The Third Hallelujah" G Lauds (daily); E Ainoi daily Orthros v. 7f. The creation (in the new day) praises the Creator (So also 149-150 below)
29	149	"The Fourth Hallelujah" G Lauds (daily); E Ainoi daily Orthros
30	150	"The Final Hallelujah" G Lauds (daily); E Ainoi daily Orthros

PSALMS AT EVENSONG

(See note and abbreviations given for "Psalms at Mattins" p. 155).

Day	Psalm	Title
1	4	"A Psalm before Bed" G and E Compline (daily) v. 9 "I will lay me down in peace"
2	6	"A Prayer for Healing" G and E Compline v. 6 "every night wash I my bed"
3	7	"An Appeal for Justice" E and P Compline v. 12 "God is provoked every day"
4	12	"Evil in Government" P Compline (Thursday; the night of intrigue) v. 1 "The faithful are vanished"
5	13	"How long?" E and G Compline v. 3 "that I sleep not in death"
6	16	"The Resurrection Psalm" P and Q Compline v. 8 "My heart teacheth me in the night season"

Day	Psalm	Title
7	31	"An Evening Commendation"
		E and G Compline
		v. 6 "Into thy hands I commend my spirit"
8	33	"The Eye of God"
		G Nocturns; Q Vespers
		v. 13 "The Lord looked down" (The eye of the night sky)
9	47	"The Clapping Psalm"
		Q Compline; G Nocturns
		v. 8 "God reigneth . . . and sitteth" (The Divine Repose)
10	51	"The Sinners' Psalm"
		G (repeated at every hour)
		v. 3 "I acknowledge my faults" (at the end of the day)
11	56	"The Psalm of Tears"
		P Compline (Friday)
		v. 1 & 5 All the day long . . .
12	73	"A Confession of Faith"
		P Nones
		v. 13 "All the day long have I been stricken"
13	86	"O Adonai"
		P Compline (Saturday)
		v. 3 "For I will call daily upon thee"
14	91	"The Guardian Angels"
		E, G and LB Compline
		v. 5 "Thou shalt not be afraid for any terror by night"
15	102	"The Lament"
		E and G Compline
		v. 3 "My days pass away like smoke"

Day	Psalm	Title
16	104	"The Glory of Nature" E Hesperinos (daily) v. 24 "Man goes to his labour until the evening"
17	117	"The Saviour of the World" E Hesperinos v. 1 "All ye nations" (An evening prayer for all humanity)
18	121	"The Travellers' Psalm" A and G Vespers v. 4 "he . . . shall neither slumber nor sleep"
19	122	"Jerusalem" G Vespers v. 7 "plenteousness within thy palaces"
20	123	"The Servants' Psalm" E Hesperinos; LB Vespers v. 2 " . . . servants" say Goodnight
21	127	"The Household Psalm" G Vespers v. 2 "the watchman"
22	130	"*De Profundis*" G, P and E Vespers v. 3 "if thou, Lord, wilt . . . mark what is done amiss" (today)
23	134	"An Evening Blessing" LB, E and G Compline v. 2 "Ye that by night stand"
24	135	"A Song of Election" G Vespers v. 7 The evening "clouds" and storms

Day	*Psalm*	*Title*

25 136 "The Great Hallel"
G Vespers
v. 9 "The moon and the stars to govern
the night"

26 137 "The Song of Babylon"
G Vespers
v. 3 "Sing us one of the songs" (the leisure
of the evening)

27 138 "The Song of Zechariah"
G Vespers; E Mesorion of Nones
v. 2 "I will worship toward thy holy
temple" (cf. Dan. 6. 10—three times
a day)

28 141 "An Evening Penitent"
G Vespers; E Hesperinos (Chrysostom)
v. 2 "the lifting up of my hands be an
evening sacrifice"

29 142 "The Prisoners' Psalm"
E Hesperinos
v. 6 "Thou art my hope" (at the end of a
bad day)

30 143 "A Penitent's Psalm"
E and G Compline
v. 8 "let me hear . . . in the morning" (of
thy Grace)

PSALMS AT THE HOLY COMMUNION

Note

Below the psalm title is suggested a "pivot" or antiphon verse and underneath that E. or G. refers to the contact in epistle or gospel where applicable.

Abbreviation

CSI indicates that the psalm is also so appointed in the Book of Common Worship (South India)

Sunday	Psalm	Title
Advent I	53	"The Foolish Body" v. 7 "Oh, that the Lord would deliver his people" E. "The day is at hand"
Advent II	85	"A Prophesy of Salvation" v. 8 "He will speak peace to his people" E. "Whatsoever things were written aforetime"
Advent III	132	"For David's Line" v. 9 "Let thy priests be clothed with righteousness" E. "stewards of the mysteries"
Advent IV	80	"The Psalm of the Vine" v. 14 "Behold, and visit this Vine" Collect "raise up . . . thy power, and come"

163

Sunday	Psalm	Title
Christmas	98	"A new song" v. 7 "Shout with joy before the Lord the King" (*Revised Psalter* 1963)
Sunday after Christmas	8	"The Creator and the Creature" v. 2 "Out of the mouth of babes" —
Epiphany	72	"The Psalm of the Epiphany" C.S.I. v. 10 "All Kings shall fall down" —
Epiphany I	122	"Jerusalem" v. 1 "We will go into the house of the Lord" G. "his parents went to Jerusalem"
Epiphany II	128	"The Wedding Psalm" v. 3 "Thy wife shall be" G. "a marriage in Cana"
Epiphany III	147	"The Second Hallelujah" v. 2 & 3 "Outcasts of Israel"— medicine G. The centurion's sick servant
Epiphany IV	81	"Festival Rejoicings and Warnings" v. 7 "At what time the storm fell" G. The stilling of the storm
Epiphany V	100	"The *Jubilate*" v. 1 "O be joyful" E. "psalms, and hymns, and spiritual songs"
Epiphany VI	95	"The *Venite*" v. 10 "It is a people that do err" G. "Gather up the tares"

Sunday	Psalm	Title
Septuagesima	121	"The Travellers' Psalm" v. 3 "He will not suffer thy foot to be moved" E. "So run that ye may obtain"
Sexagesima	107	"For those in peril" v. 10 "Fast bound in misery and iron" E. "in stripes above measure"
Quinquagesima	38	"A Psalm for Job" v. 12 "That seek after my life" G. The prediction of the Passion
Ash Wednesday	6	"A Prayer for Healing" v. 4 "Turn thee O Lord" E. "Turn ye" (Joel)
Lent I	32	"A Psalm for a Baptism" v. 4 "I was dried up" G. "forty days"
Lent II	55	"The Psalm of David" v. 1 "Hear my prayer" G. The woman of Canaan's daughter
Lent III	36	"The True Light" v. 9 "In thy light we see light" E. "Christ shall give thee light"
Lent IV	34	"A Psalm for Holy Communion" v. 8 "O taste and see" G. The feeding of the five thousand
Lent V	40	"The Sacrifice of Good Friday" v. 1 "I waited patiently" G. "took they up stones"

Sunday	Psalm	Title
Palm Sunday	118	"The Great Hosannah" CSI v. 26 "Blessed is he that comes"
Holy Week	39	"Heroic Suffering" v. 15 "O spare me a little"
Maundy Thursday	110	"The Royal Priest" v. 1 "Sit thou on my right hand"
Good Friday	22	"A Psalm for Good Friday" CSI v. 17 "They pierced my hands and my feet"
Easter Even	88	"The Saddest Psalm" v. 10 "Shall the dead rise up"
Easter	2	"The Easter Psalm" v. 6 "Have I set my King upon my holy hill"
Easter I	114	"The Exodus" v. 8 "Flintstone into a springing well" (Proper for Easter)
Easter II	23	"The Psalm of the Good Shepherd" CSI v. 1 "The Lord is my Shepherd" G. "I am the good shepherd"
Easter III	57	"The Easter Victory" v. 6 "Set up thyself O God above the heavens" G. "A little while and ye shall not see me"

Sunday	*Psalm*	*Title*
Easter IV	48	"A Psalm on Leaving" v. 8 "We wait for thy loving kind- ness" G. "the Comforter will . . . come"
Easter V	112	"An Acrostic on Man" v. 5 "A good man is merciful" E. "To visit the fatherless"
Ascension Day	24	"Gates and Doors" v. 3 "Who shall ascend" —
Sunday after Ascension	47	"The Clapping Psalm" v. 5 "God is gone up" —
Whit Sunday	68	"The Soldiers' Psalm" v. 8 "The Heavens dropped at the presence of God" —
Trinity Sunday	99	"A Psalm of God's Holiness" v. 1 "He sitteth between the Cheru- bims" E. "A door was opened in heaven"
Trinity I	146	"The First Hallelujah" v. 2 "When the breath of man goeth forth" G. Dives and Lazarus
Trinity II	145	"Thine is the Kingdom" v. 8 "The Lord is nigh all them that call upon him" G. "a great supper"
Trinity III	125	"A Psalm of Security" v. 2 "standeth the Lord round about his people" (Post Pentecost)

Sunday	*Psalm*	*Title*
Trinity IV	48	"A Psalm on Leaving"
		v. 11 "walk about Sion"
		(Post Pentecost)
Trinity V	96	"A Hymn of Praise"
		v. 10 "Tell it out among the
		heathen" (Post Pentecost)
Trinity VI	43	"Unto the altar"
(or 42 and 43)		v. 4 "I will go unto the altar"
		G. "bring thy gift to the altar"
Trinity VII	34	"A Psalm for Holy Communion"
		v. 8 "O taste, and see"
		G. The feeding of the four thousand
Trinity VIII	115	"*Non Nobis*"
		v. 1 "Not unto us"
		—
Trinity IX	105	"For Divine Guidance"
		v. 40 "He opened the rock of stone"
		E. "that Rock was Christ"
Trinity X	26	"A Psalm of Clean Hands"
		v. 8 "I have loved the habitation of
		thy house"
		G. "My house is the house of prayer"
Trinity XI	84	"The Pilgrim Psalm"
		v. 2 "a . . . longing to enter into the
		courts of the Lord"
		G. The Pharisee and the Publican
Trinity XII	103	"A Thanksgiving"
		v. 3 "forgiveth all thy sin: and
		healeth"
		G. The deaf mute

Sunday	Psalm	Title
Trinity XIII	42	"A Psalm of the Hart"
		v. 12 "My bones are smitten asunder"
		G. The Good Samaritan
Trinity XIV	116	"Rejoice with us"
		v. 1 "I am well pleased"
		G. The ten lepers
Trinity XV	119 v. 1-16	"The Law of the Lord"
Trinity XVI	119 v. 17-32	
Trinity XVII	119 v. 33-48	
Trinity XVIII	119 v. 49-64	
Trinity XIX	119 v. 65-80	
Trinity XX	119 v. 81-96	
Trinity XXI	119 v. 97-104	
Trinity XXII	119 v. 105-120	
Trinity XXIII	119 v. 125-128	
Trinity XXIV	119 v. 129-144	
Trinity XXV	65	"A Harvest Thanksgiving"
		v. 12 "Thou crownest the year"
		G. Feeding the multitude

PSALMS FOR SAINTS AND OCCASIONAL OFFICES

Note	*Abbreviations*

Below the psalm title are given the sources from whence this use has been borrowed, followed by a "pivot" or antiphon verse for this use.	LB *The Little Breviary*
	1549 ⎱ signify the Book of
	1662 ⎰ Common Prayer
	    so dated
	I India, Pakistan,
	     Burma, Ceylon 1951
	USA

Occasion	*Psalm*	*Title*
Apostles and other Saints	19	"A Psalm of Heaven" LB; I; USA (St. Paul) v. 4 "Their sound is gone out into all lands"
	111	"An Acrostic on God" LB; I v. 6 "he may give them the heritage of the heathen"
	129	"Many a time" 1549 (St. Andrew) v. 3 "The plowers plowed upon my back"
Evangelists and Missionaries	29	"The Psalm of the Voice" v. 5 "The voice of the Lord"
Martyrs	3	"The Martyrs' Song" LB v. 1 "many are they that rise against me"

Occasion	Psalm	Title
(Martyrs)	124	"The 'If' Psalm" Cyril of Alexandria etc. v. 6 "Our soul is escaped even as a bird"
Bishops, Confessors, Doctors }	15	"God's Guest" LB v. 2 "and speaketh the truth"
B.V.M. and Virgins	131	"A Psalm of Humility" 1549 (the Annunciation); U.S.A.; 1 (St. Mary Magdalene) v. 3 "even as a weaned child"
Holy Women	113	"Hallowed be Thy Name" LB v. 8 "to be a joyful mother"
Michaelmas	148	"The Third Hallelujah" 1549; I; U.S.A. v. 2 "Praise him, all ye angels"
All Saints	149	"The Fourth Hallelujah" 1549 v. 1 "let the congregation of saints praise him"
Holy Baptism and Confirmation	27	"Love of God's House" Liturgical Commission 1958 v. 4 "dwell in the house of the Lord all the days of my life"
	42/43	"The Psalm of the Hart" Ambrose for Augustine's baptism v. 1 "desireth the water brooks"

Occasion	*Psalm*	*Title*
Holy Matrimony	128	"The Wedding Psalm"
		1549
		v. 3 "Thy wife shall be . . . "
	67	"The Candlestick Psalm"
		1549
		v. 6 "shall the earth bring forth her increase"
Burial of the Dead	23	"The Psalm of the Good Shepherd"
		Gregorian and Armenian (for priest)
		v. 4 "through the valley of the shadow of death"
	90	"A Meditation at a Burial"
		1662
		v. 9 "we bring our years to an end"
	130	*"De Profundis"*
		Gregorian
		v. 1 "Out of the deep"
	139	"The Divine Indwelling"
		Gregorian
		v. 7 "if I make my bed in the grave"
		(*Revised Psalter* 1963)

These four psalms are all commended for use in *Alternative Services: Second Series* (1965).

PSALMS FOR PRIVATE RECITATION

(cf. on Withdrawal from Liturgical Use p. 105)

9 "A Psalm of Justice"
10 "A Psalm of Justice" (continued)
11 "The Coward's Chance"
18 "The Rock Psalm"
37 "The Fretting Psalm"
41 "A Sick Man's Appeal"
45 "The Spiritual Marriage"
60 "A Prayer after Disaster"
69 "A Cry from the Depths"
71 "The Old Man's Psalm"
74 "The Destruction of the Temple"
77 "A Plea for Deliverance"
78 "The Psalm of History"
79 "On Desecration"
89 "The Psalm of David"
106 "God in History"
109 "An Imprecation"
120 "The Peacemaker's Psalm"
133 "Family Unity"
140 "Against Slanderers"
144 "A Miscellany"

NOTES

CHAPTER ONE   *A Contemporary Overture*

1. *The Christian Tradition and the Unity we Seek*, A. C. Oulter p. 139, 1958 quoted in *The Renewal of Worship* edited R. C. D. Jasper p. 35 pub. O.U.P. 1965.

2. From "A Collect for Unity" appointed in Occasional Prayers in the 1928 Prayer Book of the Church of England.

3. *The Psalms in Human Life*, Rowland E. Prothero pub. Thomas Nelson and Sons 1903.

4. The theme of the year chosen by the Dean and chapter of Westminster Abbey in celebrating the 900th anniversary of dedication (December 27th 1065).

5. The Preface to the Book of Common Prayer 1662.

6. Dr. W. R. Matthews in the *Daily Telegraph* January 18th 1964.

7. *Church Music and Theology*, Eric Routley pub. Waltham Forest 1959.

8. Jasper *op. cit.* p. 21f.

9. *The Living Church*, Hans Kung pp. 195-6 pub. Sheed and Ward 1963.

10. "The Ecumenical Value of the Psalter" in *Faith and Unity* November 1964.

11. *The Readers Digest* June 1966 (from *Christianity Today*).

12. Quoted by John Huxtable, Jasper *op. cit.* p. 60.

13. *Op. cit.* p. 63.

14. *Op. cit.* p. 66 quoted from *Our Approach to God*, E. R. Micklem p. 162, 1934.

15. *Meeting for Prayer*, Dom Robert Petitpierre p. 2 pub. S.P.C.K. 1967.

16. The title chosen by Archdeacon Frank West for his book on the country parsons of Nottinghamshire pub. S.P.C.K. 1967.

17. *The Witness of the Psalms to Christ and Christianity*, W. Alexander p. 176 quoted in *The Psalms in Public Worship*, Dr. J. A. Lamb p. 160 pub. The Faith Press 1962.

18. Jasper *op. cit.* p. 28.

19. *Christian History in the Making*, Canon J. Mcleod Cambell p. 114 pub. Press and Publications Board, Westminster 1945. *The House of Kings*, edited Canon Edward Carpenter p. 289 pub. John Baker 1966.

20. Hans Kung *op. cit.* p. 421.

21. *Op. cit.* p. 214.

22. *Op. cit.* p. 227f.

23. *The History and Antiquities of the Abbey Church of St. Peter Westminster* Vol. I, Edward Wedlake Braylay p. 146 pub. J. P. Neale 1818.

24. *The Organs and Bells of Westminster Abbey*, Dr. Jocelyn Perkins, p. 10 pub. Novello 1937.

25. *The Coming Age of the Liturgical Movement* in *Studia Liturgica* Vol. II No. 4 December 1963, H. G. Hageman p. 267.

CHAPTER TWO   *The Psalms are Songs*

1. *The Early Parochial System and the Divine Office*, G. W. O. Addleshaw pp. 31–32 pub. A. R. Mowbray and Co. 1947.

2. *Psalms and Hymns in Solemn Musick*, John Playford 1671, quoted in *The Clerkes Book of 1549*, J. Wickham Legg. Henry Bradshaw Society Vol. 25, 1903 p. xx.

3. *The Makers of the Realm*, Arthur Bryant p. 133 pub. William Clowes and Sons 1955.

4. *Music in Church*, Archbishop's Committee pp. 30–31 pub. Church Information Board 1951.

5. *A Serious Call to a Devout and Holy Life*, William Law p. 157 pub. Griffith Farran Brown and Co.

6.   "Quarum tonat initium
            In tubis epulantium
            Et finis per Psalterium."
Adam of St. Victor quoted in *The Commentary on the Psalms* Vol. I. J. M. Neale and R. F. Littledale p. 2 pub. Joseph Masters and Co., 1874.

7. *St. Athanasius on the Psalms*, C.S.M.V. pub. A. R. Mowbray and Co. Ltd. 1949.

8. William Law *op. cit.* p. 169.

9. Quoted from The Psalter in *The Prayer Book Dictionary*, S. R. Driver p. 574.

10. *Reflections on the Psalms*, C. S. Lewis p. 2 pub. Geoffrey Bless 1958.

CHAPTER THREE *On the Philosophy of Sounds*

1. *Music and Religion*, Dr. W. W. Longford p. 26 pub. Kegan Paul, Trench, Trubner and Co. Ltd. 3rd ed.
2. *A History of Byzantine Music and Hymnography*, Egon Wellesz p. 47 pub. Oxford 2nd ed. 1962.
3. Aristotle *Meta* 1.5.986a. Cf. Wellesz *op. cit.* p. 48.
4. The Blessing at conclusion of the Anglican 1662 Communion Service, taken from St. Paul.
5. *Prophecy and Divination*, Dr. Alfred Guillaume p. 308 pub. Hodder and Stoughton Ltd. 1938.
6. *Op. cit.* p. 311.
7. *Op. cit.* p. 314.
8. *Op. cit.* p. 328.
9. *A History of Western Philosophy*, Bertrand Russell p. 55 pub. George Allen and Unwin Ltd. 2nd ed. 1947.
10. *Honest to God*, J. A. T. Robinson. Pub. S.C.M. Press Ltd. 1963. p. 11. "Up there or out there?"
11. c.f. *Music in the Romantic Era*, Alfred Einstein p. 350 pub. J. M. Dent and Son 1947.
12. Russell *op. cit.* p. 55 and p. 651. Jn. I. 1.
13. *The High Church Tradition*, G. W. O. Addleshaw p. 71 pub. Faber 1941.
14. Einstein *op. cit.* p. 163.
15. *Op. cit.* p. 351.
16. Here the reader may like to compare Eric Routley in *Church Music and Theology* pub. S.C.M. Press, where he describes the quality of "Innocence" in music, p. 60.

CHAPTER FOUR *"Psalms and Hymns and Spiritual Songs"*

1. *A History of Byzantine Music and Hymnography*, Egon Wellesz, p. 41 pub. O.U.P. 2nd ed. 1962.
2. *Thomas Cranmer*, Jasper Ridley, p. 16 pub. Clarendon Press 1962.
3. Cf. *Tudor Church Music*, edited E. H. Fellows, Vol. viii p. 3 etc. pub. O.U.P. 1925.
4. Wellesz *op. cit.* p. 147.
5. Compare Frere's note on p. 5, *Hymns Ancient and Modern* Historical Edition pub. William Clowes 1909.
6. Wellesz *op. cit.* p. 165f.
7. Wellesz *op. cit.* p. 45.

8. Wellesz *op. cit.* p. 34f.
9. *St. Paul and the Church of the Gentiles*, Dr. Wilfred Knox p. 9 pub. C.U.P. 1961.
10. *The Psalms in Christian Worship*, Dr. J. A. Lamb p. 25 pub. The Faith Press 1962.
11. *The High Church Tradition*, G. W. O. Addleshaw p. 90.
12. Lamb *op. cit.* p. 35f.
13. *The Rock and the River*, Martin Thornton p. 45 and p. 52, pub. Hodder and Stoughton 1960.
14. Thornton *op. cit.* p. 100 and p. 60.

CHAPTER FIVE   *Church and Synagogue*

1. *The Influence of the Synagogue upon the Divine Office*, C. W. Dugmore p. 49 pub. The Faith Press Ltd. 1964.
2. *Op. cit.* pp. 47-52.
3. *Op. cit.* p. 56. Also note *The Early Liturgy*, J. A. Jungmann p. 278 pub. Darton, Longman and Todd 1960: "It will come as a surprise to many no doubt to note that the eucharistic celebration did not occupy the prominent place which it has at present."
4. *English Spirituality*, Martin Thornton p. 280 pub. S.P.C.K. 1963.
5. Dugmore *op. cit.* p. 70.
6. *Op. cit.* p. 95.
7. *Op. cit.* p. 97.
8. *Op. cit.* p. 98.
9. *The Idea of the Holy*, Rudolph Otto p. 25 Penguin Edition 1959.
10. *The High Church Tradition*, G. W. O. Addleshaw p. 89.
11. Dugmore *op. cit.* p. 110-113.
12. *Op. cit.* p. 78.
13. *The Sacred Bridge*, Eric Werner pub. Denis Dobson 1959. (The Interdependence of Liturgy and Music in Synagogue and Church during the First Millenium) p. 11.
14. *Op. cit.* p. 22.
15. *Op. cit.* p. 144.
16. Tertullian Apol. 39.
17. Eusebius on Psalm 91 (P.G. XXIII, 1172).
18. Werner *op. cit.* p. 148.
19. *Op. cit.* p. 323.
20. *Op. cit.* p. 324.

21. *Op. cit.* p. 325.
22. *Op. cit.* p. 145.

CHAPTER SIX   *Cranmer and the Reform*

1. The preface in the Book of Common Prayer "Concerning the Service of the Church 1549".
2. *The Shape of the Liturgy*, Gregory Dix p. 330 pub. Dacre Press Westminster 2nd ed. 1945.
3. W. C. Bishop on "The Liturgical Use of the Psalter" in *The Prayer Book Dictionary* pub. Waverley Book Co. Ltd., London.
4. *St. Augustine's Lectionary*, G. G. Willis p. 7 pub. S.P.C.K. London 1962.
5. St. Augustine on Psalm 138, quoted from *Christian Antiquities*, Blackamore p. 110 pub. E. Bell 1722.
6. *Christian Worship*, Mgr. L. Duchesne, p. 169 pub. S.P.C.K. 5th ed. 1919.
7. *The Early Liturgy*, J. A. Jungmann p. 287.
8. G. G. Willis *op. cit.* p. 21.
9. St. Hilary on Psalm 65 quoted in *A Summary of Christian Antiquities*, Blackamore p. 52 Vol. II.
10. Quoted from *Commentary on the Psalms*, J. M. Neale and R. F. Littledale, Vol. I p. 5 pub. Joseph Masters and Co., London 1874.
11. Book of Common Prayer "Concerning the Service of the Church" 1549.
12. J. M. Neale *op. cit.* p. 10.
13. J. M. Neale *op. cit.* p. 22.
14. *The Troubadours and England*, Dr. H. C. Chaytor, p. 3 pub. C.U.P. 1923.

Part of this chapter is from my article "The Parish, the People and the Psalms", published in *Parish and People* Michaelmas 1962 and reprinted here with permission.

CHAPTER SEVEN   *Aspects of the Office in the Eighteenth Century*

1. Hooper's MS. quoted in *The English Church in the Eighteenth Century*, C. J. Abbey and J. H. Overton p. 443 pub. Longman's Green and Co. 1887.
2. *Gentleman's Magazine* Vol. lxix, 667, quoted Abbey and Overton *op. cit.* p. 416.

3. *Hymnody Past and Present*, C. S. Phillips p. 170 pub. S.P.C.K. 1937.

4. Abbey and Overton *op. cit.* p. 87.

5. *Compton, the Protestant Bishop*, Edward Carpenter p. 242, 247f.

6. Chapter Act May 6th 1710, quoted in *The Westminster Abbey Singers*, Edward Pine p. 139 and p. 150 pub. Denis Dobson 1953.

7. *Cathedral Music*, William Boyce 2nd ed. 1788.

8. *English Cathedral Music*, E. H. Fellows p. 32 pub. Methuen 1941.

9. *The House of Kings, the Official History of Westminster Abbey.* Cf. pp. 109, 114, 134, 210, 419 etc. pub. John Baker, London 1966. On the evening of July 6th 1966, a similar event took place when Her Majesty the Queen "with her consort was dining with the Collegiate Body of St. Peter in Westminster . . . a homely occasion". MS. in Westminster Abbey *Occasional Paper* Winter 1966.

10. *English Spirituality*, Martin Thornton, p. 273 pub. S.P.C.K. 1963.

11. *Nashdon Abbey Record* Autumn 1964.

12. *The Singing Church*, C. H. Phillips p. 17 Faber and Faber 1945. Also Edward Pine *op. cit.* p. 135.

13. *Lancelot Andrewes 1555–1626*, Paul A. Welsby p. 202f. pub. S.P.C.K. 1958.

14. Abbey and Overton *op. cit.* p. 443.

15. *A History of the Church of England*, J. R. H. Moorman, p. 271 and p. 323 pub. Adam and Charles Black 1953.

16. Abbey and Overton *op. cit.* p. 412f. and p. 460.

17. "Sermon at the Three Choirs Festival, 7th September 1720", published in *A Rationale on Cathedral Music*, Thomas Bisse D.D., 1720.

18. *Medieval Services in England*, Christopher Wordsworth pub. T. Baker 1898.

English Church Life, Wickham Legg, p. 80 and p. 82 pub. Longmans Green and Co. 1914.

The High Church Tradition, G. W. O. Addleshaw p. 62 pub. Faber and Faber 1941.

19. *Pastoral Liturgy*, J. A. Jungmann, p. 112 and p. 152 pub. Challoner 1963.

20. C. H. Phillips *op. cit.* p. 108.

21. Abbey and Overton *op. cit.* p. 429f.

22. *Hymns and Spiritual Songs in Three Books,* Isaac Watts 1707.
23. *The England of Elizabeth,* A. L. Rowse, p. 484f. pub. Macmillan 1950. Reprint Society Edition 1953.
24. *Anglican Liturgies of the Seventeenth and Eighteenth Centuries,* edited W. Jardine Grisbrooke p. 38 pub. S.P.C.K. 1958.
25. "A cherished part of our heritage in the Anglican Communion is the Book of Common Prayer, which is a bond of unity between us and which provides the forms whereby we live the life of the Catholic Church."
Lambeth Conference 1958 Encyclical Letter p. 1 and p. 25 pub. S.P.C.K. Seabury 1958.
26. *Ordinale Exon.* pub. Henry Bradshaw Society.
27. Bishops Kennet's *Life* 1730 p. 126. Brokesby's *Life of Dodwell,* p. 359 and p. 369. Cf. Abbey and Overton *op. cit.* p. 458.
28. William Boyce *op. cit.*
29. *The Organs and Bells of Westminster Abbey,* Jocelyn Perkins p. 29 pub. Novello and Co. Ltd. 1937.
30. Perkins *op. cit.* p. 31f.
31. *The House of Kings,* *op. cit.* p. 242.

CHAPTER EIGHT   *Aspects of the Office in the Nineteenth Century*

1. *St. Paul's in its Glory (1831-1911),* G. L. Prestige p. 2 pub. S.P.C.K. 1955.
2. *Op. cit.* p. 3 and p. 5.
3. *Op. cit.* p. 4, p. 9 and p. 11.
4. Edward Pine *op. cit.* p. 193f.
5. Perkins *op. cit.* p. 43f. and p. 49.
   House of Kings op. cit. p. 109 and p. 113.
6. *House of Kings op cit.* p. 296.
7. *Reply to the Cathedral Commissioners,* S. S. Wesley p. 6 pub. Piper, Stevenson and Spence, London 1853.
8. *Cathedral Music and the Musical System of the Church,* S. S. Wesley p. 8 pub. F. J. Rivington, London 1849.
9. *Cathedral Trusts and their Fulfillment,* Robert Whiston p. 41 pub. John Olliver, London 1849.
10. *Lecture on Church Music,* William Spark p. 17 pub. R. Slocombe, Leeds 1851.
11. *Parochial Psalmody,* W. H. H. Paper read to the Shrewsbury Ruri Decanal Chapter, pub. F. and J. Rivington, London 1851.
12. *Reformation of Cathedral Music,* Anon. p. 21f. pub. F. and J. Rivington, London 1849.

13. *A Short History of the Oxford Movement*, S. L. Ollard p. 200 pub. A. R. Mowbray and Co. 1915.

14. Wickham Legg *op. cit.* p. 106.

15. Prestige *op. cit.* p. 93f.

16. Edward Pine *op. cit.* p. 233f.

17. *Towards a More Prayerful Liturgy*, Dom L. Leloir, O.S.B., *Sobornost* p. 13. Series 5, No. 1 p. 39 pub. Faith Press.

18. Compare here "Mind-closers". "It is far better to leave them on their knees . . . " etc. Dom Robert Petitpierre *op. cit.* p. 8.

19. *The Rock and the River*, Martin Thornton, p. 110 pub. Hodder and Stoughton.

20. *Sussex Church Music in the Past*, K. H. Macdermott, Rector of Selsey, p. 52 pub. Moore and Wingham, Chichester 2nd ed.

21. Prestige *op. cit.* p. 147.

CHAPTER NINE   *Parson, People and the Opus Dei in the Twentieth Century*

1. Dom Lelois *op. cit.* p. 38.

2. *The Dynamics of Liturgy*, H. A. Reinhold, pub. Collier-Macmillan 1961. Quoted by permission of the Macmillan Company.

3. *The Living Church*, Hans Kung. English Edition p. 191f. pub. Sheed and Ward 1963.

4. *Vision of Peace: A Study in Benedictine Monastic Life* (1963), Dom Wilfred Tuninek, p. 319 (quoted in *Sobornost* Summer 1965).

5. *The Little Breviary*, ed. The Nuns of Stanbrook pub. Burns and Oates 1958.

6. *The Liturgy of the Word*, Josef Jungman, S.J., p. 75 and p. 65 pub. Burns and Oates 1966.

7. Ambrose (Orat cont Auxent Ep. 32) quoted in Blackamore's *Christian Antiquities* Vol. II, p. 55 pub. E. Bell, London 1722.

8. *Pastoral Theology*, Josef Jungman, S.J. p. 152 pub. Challoner 1963.

9. Reinhold *op. cit.*

10. *Life Together*, Dietrich Bonhoeffer, p. 47f. pub. S.C.M. Press 1954.

11. H. A. Reinhold *op. cit.*

12. *The Taizé Office* p. 436 pub. Faith Press. English Edition 1966.

13. *A Liturgical Psalter*, Walter Howard Frere p. viii. pub. A. R. Mowbray and Co. Ltd. 1925.

14. *Pastoral Liturgy*, Jungmann, p. 210.

15. *The Place of Bonhoeffer*, edited Martin E. Martz, p. 182 pub. S.C.M. Press.

16. *Pastoral Liturgy*, Jungmann, p. 381.

17. Frere *op. cit.* p. iv.

18. Dietrich Bonhoeffer *op. cit.* p. 47f.

19. *Practical Plainsong*, Dom Aldhelm Dean.

20. *Some Principles of Liturgical Reform*, W. H. Frere p. 82 pub. John Murray 2nd ed. 1914.

21. *Prayer Book Revision in England 1800-1900*, R. C. D. Jasper p. 61 and p. 80 pub. S.P.C.K. 1954.

CHAPTER TEN   *A Psalter Arranged for Song*

1. J. M. Neale *op. cit.* p. 34.

2. *The Book of Common Worship* pub. O.U.P. Cf. p. 100 and 23f.

3. *A Proposed Prayer Book* (India, Pakistan, Burma, and Ceylon), pub. S.P.C.K., Madras 1952.

4. The Book of Common Prayer (Protestant Episcopal Church U.S.A.) pub. The Church Pension Fund, New York 1945.

5. *A Liturgical Psalter*, W. H. Frere pub. A. R. Mowbray Ltd. 1925.

6. *The High Church Tradition*, G. W. O. Addleshaw p. 49.
Some Principles of Liturgical Reform, W. H. Frere p. 85.

7. *The Holy Eucharist* pub. Church in Wales Publications, 8 Mitcham Road, Penarth 1966.

8. Robert Bridges' article on Chanting in *The Prayer Book Dictionary* p. 181 pub. the Waverley Book Co. Ltd.

I am indebted in this chapter to *Prism* for permission to reproduce material from my article published in No. 66 October 1962.

9. *The Paragraph Psalter arranged for the use of choirs*, Dr. B. F. Westcott pub. O.U.P. 1912.

10. *The Worcester Psalter*, Sir Ivor Atkins pub. Adam and Charles Black 1950.

11. *The Revised Psalter* (printed for use with Anglican chants) pub. S.P.C.K. etc. London, 1966.

12. *The Clerkes Book of 1549*, J. Wickham Legg.

13. *The Anglican Chant Book* pub. Novello and Co., 1955.

14. *Opus Tertium* (LXXII) 1267, Roger Bacon.
15. *Merbeckes Book of Common Prayer Noted* 1550 ed. J. E. Hunt pub. S.P.C.K. London and Macmillan N.Y. 1939.
16. *Reflections on the Psalms*, C. S. Lewis pub. Geoffrey Bles 1958.
17. *Truth, Unity and Concord*, C. Kenneth Sansbury, Mowbrays, 1967.
18. *The War-Songs of the Prince of Peace*, R. M. Benson p. 10 pub. John Murray 1901.
19. Dr. Kenneth Sansbury *op. cit.*
20. C. S. Lewis *op. cit.* p. 22.
21. *The Psalms in Israel's Worship*, Sigmund Mowinckel Vol. I p. 13. and p. 5, Vol. II p. 31 pub. (English Translation) Basil Black 1962.
22. Mowinckel *op. cit.* Vol. I p. 8.
23. Mowinckel *op cit.* Vol. II p. 82.
24. *According to the Scriptures*, C. H. Dodd p. 108f. pub. Nisbet and Co., London 1952.

CHAPTER ELEVEN *Worship in the Age of Din*

1. *The Idea of the Holy*, Rudolph Otto (1917). Pelican Edition 1959, p. 85.
2. Otto *op. cit.* p. 21.
3. Otto *op. cit.* p. 168.
4. Otto *op. cit.* p. 30.
5. *Music in the Life of Man*, Julius Portnoy, p. 199 pub. Holt, Rinehart and Winstone Ltd. 1963.
6. *Therapeutic and Industrial Uses of Music*, Doris Soibelman p. 176 Columbia University Press, New York 1948.
7. *Music as a Supplement in Nitrous Oxide-Oxygen* Anaesthesia, Harry Cheery and Irving M. Pullen 1947. Cf. Doris Soibelman *op. cit.* p. 172.
8. Cf. *Politics* 1339, *Laws* 11668. Quoted *A History of Byzantine Music and Hymnography*, Egon Wellesz p. 50 and p. 51 pub. O.U.P. 2nd ed. 1962.
9. Portnoy *op. cit.* p. 201.

CHAPTER TWELVE *Theological Considerations in Liturgical Reform*

1. Reginald Fuller in *The Place of Bonhoeffer* op. cit. p. 176.
2. *Liturgy Coming to Life*, John Robinson pub. Mowbray 1960.

3. "Cathedrals in the Twentieth Century", R. C. Moore in *English Church Music* p. 9 pub. R.S.C.M. Adlington Palace, 1965.

4. *The English Secular Cathedrals in the Middle Ages*, Kathleen Edwards Manchester University Press 1949.

5. *Roger Bacon Opera*, Vol. I, edited J. S. Brewer p. 297 pub. Longman Green Longman Roberts 1859. (Opus Tertium Chapter 72) "*Sed iam per ecclesiam paulatim crevit abusus cantus . . .*"

6. Edward Pine *op. cit.* p. 120.

7. *Orlando Gibbons*, E. H. Fellows p. 44 O.U.P. 1925.

8. *On the Choral Service*, J. Jebb p. 151f. 1843.

9. *The Twentieth Century Cathedral*, H. C. N. Williams p. 18 pub. Hodder and Stoughton.

10. Dr. P. C. Moore *op. cit.* p. 12.

11. R. Otto *op. cit.* p. 76.

12. "Principles", Frere *op. cit.* p. 167.

13. Cf. here Frere *op. cit.* p. 179 where he appeals for a return to the liturgical anthem.

14. *Divine Services and Anthems*, James Clifford 1663. See also here p. 141f. and 207f. of *Music and the Reformation in England, 1549-1660.*—Dr. Peter Le Huray pub. Herbert Jenkins 1967. Unfortunately this most valuable study was not available to me at the time of going to print.

15. *Music by Lloyd Webber* pub. 1959.

16. *Pastoral Liturgy*, J. A. Jungmann *op. cit.* p. 188.

17. Cf. here Frere "Principles" *op. cit.* p. 147.

18. *The High Church Tradition*, G. W. O. Addleshaw *op. cit.* p. 94.

19. Edward Pine *op. cit.* p. 55.

20. Quoted by Paul A. Welsby *Lancelot Andrewes 1555-1626* p. 75 pub. S.P.C.K. 1958.

21. Cf. *The House of Kings, op. cit.* p. 462.

CHAPTER THIRTEEN *Concerning "Common Prayer"*

1. This quotation is taken from the medieval studies of G. A. Coulton. I regret I cannot now trace its exact location.

2. *English Spirituality*, Martin Thornton, p. 258.

3. Werner *op. cit.* p. 27.

4. *The Rock and the River*, Martin Thornton p. 45f.

5. *Life and Liturgy*, Louis Bouyer p. 243 pub. Sheed and Ward 1956.

6. *The Work of God*, C.S.M.V., Chapter IV and p. 54 pub. Faith Press 1964.

7. Dugmore *op. cit.* p. 71.

8. Bouyer *op. cit.* p. 230.

9. *The Rock and the River*, Martin Thornton p. 102.

10. *The Prayer Book Dictionary*—article on chanting by Robert Bridges, p. 181.

11. Cf. *The Rock and the River*, Martin Thornton p. 114.

12. *Worship and Mission*, Rupert E. Davies p. 69 and p. 74 pub. S.C.M. Press 1966.

13. Dom L. Leloir *op. cit.* p. 44.

14. *The Whole Man at Worship*, Helene Lubienska de Lenval pp. 75, 63, 55. English Edition Geoffrey Chapman, London 1961.

15. *The High Church Tradition*, G. W. O. Addleshaw p. 77.

16. *A Serious Call to a Devout and Holy Life*, William Law, Chapter XV

17. *Missionary Heroes in Africa*, Dr. J. C. Lambert p. 40 pub. Seeley and Co. Ltd. 1909.

18. Louis Bouyer *op. cit.* p. 47.

INDEX

Abbey and Overton, 178f.
Adam of St. Victor, 30, 175
Addleshaw, G. W. O., 26, 38, 96, 108, 175, 176, 177, 179, 182, 184, 185.
Aidan, St., 28
Alcuin, 129
Alexander, W., 19, 174
Alexandrinus, Codex, 142
Algazel, 36
Ambrose, Bp. of Milan, 56f., 74, 96, 181
American, Journal of Psychiatry, 125
Andrews, Bp. Lancelot, 72, 143, 179, 184
Anne, Queen, 77
Anselm, St., 33
Anthem, 135
Apostolic Tradition, 53
Aquinas, St. Thomas, 37, 62
Aristotle, 33, 125, 176
Armenia, 62
Articles, Thirty Nine, 56
Arze, John of, 99
Athanasius, St., 30
Atkins, Sir Ivor, 182
Attwood, Thomas, 81, 85
Augustine, St., (Hippo) 41, 54, 56f., 73, 74, 96, 107
Augustine's St., (College), 20
Augustine's St., (Lectionary), 64, 178

Bach, J. S., 121

Bacon, Roger, 113, 130, 183, 184
Basil, St., 41
Baxter, Richard, 75
Bede, The Ven., 129
Beethoven, 37
Benedictines, 71, 145
Benson, R. M., 117, 183
Berne, Monks of, 95, 102, 109
Berwick, (Sussex), 91
Binney, Thomas, 16
Bishop, W. C., 63, 178
Bisse, Dr. Thomas, 73, 179
Blackamore, Christian Antiquities, 178, 181
Bonhoeffer, D., 51, 97, 99, 181, 182
Book of Common Worship, (C.S.I.), 104
Bouyer, Louis, 147, 151, 185
Boyce, William, 70, 72, 76, 179, 180
Brahmins, 32
Brayley, E. W., 175
Bridge, Sir Frederick, 83
Bridges, Robert, 182, 185
British Broadcasting Corporation, 124
British Journal, 79
Brown, Thomas, 71
Bryant, Arthur, 28, 175
Byrd, William, 44, 128, 137

Campbell, J. M., 175
Canterbury, Archbishop of, 148

Canterbury, Cathedral, 68
Canticles, 135, 142
Carpenter, Canon Edward, 175, 179
Catherine's, St. (College), 33
Cathedral, Psalter, 91
Chapel, Royal, 138
Chase, Dr. G. A., 58
Chaytor, Dr. H. C., 178
Chevatogne, 17
Chichester, 130
Chrysostom, St. John, 30, 56f., 74
Clement, St. (of Alexandria), 109
Clifford, James, 136f., 184
Columba, St., 28
Compton, Bp. of London, 69, 179
Constantinople, Council of, 46
Convocation, 101
Coulton, G. A., 184
Coventry, 132
Coverdale, Bp., 31
Cranmer, Archbishop, 26, 28, 42, 55, 60, 63f.
Croft, William, 78
C.S.M.V., 146, 175, 184
Cushing, Cardinal, 17
Cyprian, St., 54
Cyril of Jerusalem, 107

Davies, Rupert E., 148, 185
Dean, Dom Aldhelm, 100, 182
Descartes, 37
Dix, Dom Gregory, 63, 178
Dodd, Prof. C. H., 183
Dodwell, 77, 180
Driver, Prof. C. R., 175
Dugmore, Dr. C. W., 53, 58, 177, 185
Dunstan, St., 28
Duschene, Mgr. L., 64, 178
Dykes, Dr. J. B., 33, 91

Ebdon, Thomas, 70
Ecstasy, 35f.

Edward, King and Confessor, 46
Edward VI, 28
Edwards, Dr. Kathleen, 129, 184
Egyptians, 32
Einstein, Alfred, 176
Elisha, 35
Elizabeth I, 71
Elliot, Charlotte, 123
Eusebius, 177

Fellowes, Dr. E. H., 131, 176, 179, 184
Ferrar, Nicholas, 76
Flintoft, Luke, 76, 114
Frere, Bp. Walter, 98f., 105, 182, 184
Freud, Sigmund, 139
Fuller, Reginald, 128, 183

Gelineau, Joseph, 103
"Gentleman's Magazine", 178
George II, (Coronation of), 79
George's St., (Cathedral), 82f., 86
Gibbons, Orlando, 23, 44, 130, 136f., 184
Gloria in Excelsis, 46
Goss, Dr. John, 88, 138
Grandisson, Bp. Jean de, 77
Gray, Bp. Robert, 21
Gregory, Canon Robert, 88
Grisbrooke, E. J., 180
Guillaume, Dr. A., 35f., 176
Gurney, Edmund, 37

Hackett, John, 143
Hageman, H. G., 25, 175
Hale, Archdeacon, 88
Handel, G. F., 79
Hannington, Bp. of Uganda, 20
Hanslick, Eduard, 39
Hawkins, Sir John, 78
Hazelton, Roger, 16
Henry III, 79
Henry VIII, 70

Herbert, George, 57
Hertz, Dr. J., 17
Hilary, St., 51, 65, 74
Hunt, J. E., 183
Hunter, Bp. Leslie, 93
Huray, Dr. Peter Le, 184
Huxtable, John, 174
Hymns, 45, 75

Industrial Revolution, 20
Ireland, John, 83

James, Master of Song, 129
Jasper, Dr. R. C. D., 174, 182
Jebb, John, 83, 184
Jerome, St., 65
John XXIII, Pope, 17
Jungmann, J., 74, 95, 139, 177,
    178, 179, 181, 182, 184
Justinian, 46

Keble, John, 88
Keene, Henry, 80
Ken, Bp, T., 46, 68, 74
Kennet, Bp. of Peterborough,
    180
King's College, Cambridge, 40
Knox, Dr. Wilfred, 48, 177
Kung, Hans, 17, 22, 94, 174,
    175, 181
Kyrie, 139

Lamb, Dr. J. A., 16, 19, 50,
    174, 177
Lambert, Dr. J. C., 185
Lambeth, Conference, 28, 77,
    180
Laodicaea, Council of, 45, 50,
    107
Laud, Abp. of Canterbury, 141
Law, William, 29, 31, 74, 150,
    175, 185.
Legg, J. Wickham, 175, 179,
    181
Lelois, Dom L., 93, 181, 185
Lewis, C. S., 31, 116f., 175, 183
Liddon, Canon H. P., 88f.

Lincoln, Cathedral, 37, 127,
    129, 131
Liszt, Franz, 38f.
Little Breviary (see Monks of
    Berne)
Little Gidding, 76
Locke, John, 37
Longford, Dr. W. W., 176
Lubienska de Lenval, Helêne,
    149, 185

Ma'amad, 53, 146
Macdermott, K. H., 181
Mackenzie, Bp. Charles F., 20
Mary, Queen, 68
Mathews, Dr. W. R., 16, 174
Medical Research Council, 123
Mendelssohn, Felix, 82
Merbecke, John, 114, 130
Michal, 35
Micklem E. R., 174
Moffat, J. S., 151
Monophysites, 46
Montini, Cardinal, 95
Moore, Dr. P. C., 129, 133,
    143, 184
Moorman, Dr. J. R. H., 179
Moule, Prof. C. D. F., 116
Mowinckel, Sigmund, 118f.,
    183

Nashdom, 71, 179
Neale, J. M., 101, 103, 175, 178
Nicea, Council of, 61
Nicomachus, of Geraca, 33
Norwich, Dean of, 101

Occasional Offices, 109, 170
Ollard, S. L., 181
"One People", 16
Organ, 77f.
Origen, 41, 54, 107
Orthodox, 18, 46, 66
Othello, 125
Otto, Rudolf, 57, 121f., 177,
    183, 184
Oulter, A. C., 15, 174

Owen, John, 18
Oxford Movement, 26, 87

"Parish and People", 178
Parker, Abp. of Canterbury, 131
Patrick, Bp. of Ely, 74
Patrick, St., 28
Patterson, Bp. J. C., 20
Paul the Silentiary, 47
Paul, St., 41f.
Paul's, St. (Cathedral), 72, 81f.
Pearce, Dean Zachary, 71
Perkins, Dr. Jocelyn, 78, 175, 180
Perry, Bp. Charles, 21
Peter's, St. (Day), 21
Petit Pierre, Dom Robert, 18, 174, 181
Phillimore, Sir Robert, 81
Phillips, C. H., 179
Phillips, C. S., 179
Pine, Edward, 179, 180, 184
Plato, 126
Playford, John, 28, 175
Plotinus, 38
Portnoy, Julius, 126, 183
Posadas, Bp. of, 146
Prestige, G. L., 180f.
"Prism", 182
Prothero, R. E., 15, 174
Purcell, Henry, 138
Pythagoras, 36

Quignon, Cardinal, 66, 99, 102, 106

Reinhold, H. A., 94, 181
Revised Psalter, 112
Reynolds, Wynford, 124
Ridley, J., 176
Riley, Harold, 100, 142
Robinson, Bp. J. A. T., 36, 39, 176, 183
Robinson, John, (Organist), 78f., 128
Roman Catholic, 16, 18

Rousseau, Dom Olivier, 17
Routley, Dr. Erik, 16, 174, 176
Rouse, A. L., 76, 180
Royal School of Church Music, 26
Russell, Bertrand, 36f., 176

Sancroft, Abp., 75
Sansbury, Bp. C. K., 116, 183
Savoy, 31
Schrider, Organ, 79
Short, Bp. Augustus, 21
Shrewsbury, 180
"Singing Church", 151
Smith, Sidney, 81
Sobornost, 181
Soibelman, Doris, 183
Sophia, St. (Cathedral), 46
Spark, William, 86, 180
Spencer, Edmund, 139
"Spiritual Songs", 41f.
Stainer, John, 39, 88
Stanbrook, Nuns of, 181
Stanford, C. V., 115
Stevens, John, 76
Synagogue, 53, 55, 58

Taizé, Community of, 93
Tallis, Thomas, 44, 70, 78, 130
Taylor, Jeremy, 68
Te Deum, 46, 142, 144
Tenbury, St. Michael's, 141
Tertullian, 57, 63, 177
Teutonic, Christianity, 19
"Theology", Journal of, 93, 116
Thornton, Dr. Martin, 52, 55, 71, 91, 144, 177, 179, 181, 185
Thoresby, Ralph, 73
Tillich, Paul, 52
Tindal, Matthew, 69
Toledo, Council of, 74
Tomkins, Thomas, 44
Trench, Dean, 84
Tuninek, Dom Wilfred, 94, 181
Trinity Church, Coventry, 112

Troubadours, 67, 178
Tudway, Dr. Thomas, 78
Turle, James, 83
Turner, Bp. of Ely, 74
Tuxeda, John, 23
Tye, Christopher, 130, 137
Tyrrell, Bp. William, 21

Vatican Council, 22, 146
Veni, Creator, 46

Walpole, Sir Robert, 79
Watts, Isaac, 69, 75, 180
Weelkes, Thomas, 136
Wellesz, Dr. Egon, 41f., 47, 175
183
Welsby, Dr. Paul A., 179, 184

Werner, Prof. Eric, 60, 177, 184
Wesley, John, 72
Wesley, Samuel Sebastian, 84f.,
180
West, Frank, 174
Westborne, Rector of, 88
Westcott, Bp. B. F., 111, 182
Westminster Abbey, 18, 21, 23,
25, 39, 46, 68f., 82f., 130, 179
Whiston, Robert, 86, 180
Williams, C. N., 184
Williams, Dean, 23
Willis, Dr. G. G., 64, 178
Worcester, Psalter, 42
Wordsworth, Bp. Christopher,
127, 179
Wren, Sir Christopher, 78